EDEN REVISITED

A NOVEL BY
LASZLO Z. BITO

Foreword by Bruce Chilton

Afterword by Ágnes Heller

NATUS BOOKS
BARRYTOWN, NY

INSTITUTE OF ADVANCED THEOLOGY
BARD COLLEGE
ANNANDALE-ON-HUDSON, NY

© 2022 The Estate of Laszlo Z. Bito
Translated by Amy Modly
Edited by John Solomon

All rights reserved. Except for short passages for purposes of review, no part of this book may be reproduced in any form or by any means, electronic or mechanical, including photocopying, recording, or by any information storage and retrieval system, without permission in writing from the publisher.

Published by Natus Books, 120 Station Hill Road, Barrytown, NY 12507; and the Institute of Advanced Theology, Bard College, Campus Road, PO Box 5000 Annandale-on-Hudson, New York 12504

Natus Books is a publishing project of the Institute for Publishing Arts, a not-for-profit, tax-exempt organization [501(c)(3)].

First published in 2009 by Argumentum Kiado, Budapest.

Cover and interior design by Stacy Wakefield Forte
Cover: Currier & Ives (firm), "Adam and Eve in the Garden of Eden" (1848), hand colored lithograph, 10"×14".

ISBN: 978-1-581772-16-6

Library of Congress Control Number: 2022931452

Manufactured in the United States of America

*With heartfelt thanks to
John Solomon—mentor,
editor, friend. And to his dear
wife, Ruth Solomon, for her
invaluable support.*

CONTENTS

Foreword by Bruce Chilton ix

Eden Revisited

PART I: In Defense of Cain 2

PART II: Cain in the Land of Nód 38

PART III: Cain's Return to the World of His Parents 132

Afterword by Ágnes Heller 239

About Bruce Chilton 251

About Ágnes Heller 252

About the Institute of Advanced Theology 253

About Natus Books 254

About the Author 255

FOREWORD

IN *EDEN REVISITED*, Laszlo Z. Bito reimagines the biblical story of Adam, Eve, and their children, Cain and Abel, in vibrant detail. In Bito's version, Abel—who is barely mentioned in the Bible, which tells us only that he was a shepherd and that God appreciated his animal sacrifice more than his older brother's offering of grain—is far from the innocent victim of conventional theology. Because Abel became a herder in a wilderness region prior to domestication, that meant he must have trapped animals—and Bito imagines that, one day, he used a trap to ensnare his father Adam.

This outbreak of violence against Adam is motivated by sexual jealousy. Abel says to his father, in regard to Eve, "You alone can't possess the only woman our Lord created." With very good reason, Ágnes Heller, in her Afterword to this book, observes that Sigmund Freud is one of the influences on this strange new narrative. Sexuality is constantly in play within the novel, but it does not manifest as a simple, primal instinct. Rather, the inextricably related issues of the subjugation of women and the desire to subjugate in itself are what concern Bito.

The novel investigates the darkness of human passion. At the same time, Bito's response is not fearful. The author was compelled to work in a mine as a young man when Hungary was under Soviet rule in the 1950s; he valued protest as a response to oppression. So his Cain intervenes in Abel's attack on Adam, which begins Cain's odyssey to both free himself and to understand himself.

Bito lovingly traces Cain's growth and maturation. He is not the perpetual vagrant of Genesis but a person yearning to fulfil his humanity. His only useful weapon—humanity's only useful weapon—against the violence around us and within us, is knowledge. Bito is convinced that the tree which produced knowledge cannot have been evil; the human blight is too little, not too much.

I once remarked in conversation with Laszlo Bito that he appreciated knowledge in the sense that the ancient Gnostics did. They and he see knowledge (*gnosis*) not as the result of accumulated perceptions about the world as it is, but as direct insight into the nature of the world as it should be. A true Gnostic cultivates the knowledge that makes us free, which is what both Cain and Eve do; and, after much stubborn protest, Adam does as well. Bito's characters reflect his own gnostic quest, leading him to reinvent Cain as the progenitor of how we might reimagine ourselves as a people and a civilization.

>   Bruce Chilton
>   Bernard Iddings Bell Professor of Philosophy and Religion, Bard College

AND THE LORD
SET A MARK
UPON CAIN,
LEST ANY
FINDING HIM
SHOULD KILL HIM.

GENESIS 4:15

I

In Defense *of* Cain

ONE

PEACE REIGNED FOR many years throughout the forests and fields beyond the gates of Eden, Adam's Outerworld, the name he had given to the boundless expanse under his protection. He mused about how he would one day be lord over this richly flowering land that stretched from the Gihon River to the swamps of Ai.

His only human companion, Eve, who was like a sister to him growing up and who the Lord of the Garden intended to be his woman, pined even more than Adam for the freedom of the Outerworld. It was a relief when, after they ate from the fruit of the forbidden tree, their Lord himself led them from his Garden into the Outerworld, putting Adam in charge of all. True, he did sentence Adam to earn his bread by the sweat of his brow, but Adam didn't mind hard work: it banished the boredom he had felt in Eden.

Eve, on the other hand, regretted that the Lord increased the pain of her childbearing with his curse because of her disobedience. Her growing belly filled the motherless girl with fear as, knowing nothing of woman's fate, she couldn't imagine how the fruit of her womb was going to be plucked from her body.

She was even more concerned when the Lord's curse placed her under her husband's dominion. Eve considered herself equal to Adam in every way and couldn't accept this. It wasn't until years after their firstborn, Cain, came into the world, followed by a long period of hoping for a girl, that serenity settled in the parents' hearts. Adam believed so fully in the all-encompassing wisdom of their Lord that he didn't notice, or didn't wish to notice, the growing tension as their second son, Abel, grew to manhood in the world of only one woman. He considered it an unfortunate accident when, while walking in the woods one day, a trailing vine trapped him, yanking him into the air by his ankle.

"Where are you, Abel?" Adam called. "Come quick, before some beast attacks me! Your trap ensnared me instead of a ram!"

Abel cautiously approached his father, his heavy club at shoulder level.

"That ram is you, Father. I set the trap for you! You alone can't possess the only woman our Lord created."

Abel struck his father with his maul. It would have been a lethal blow if Adam hadn't protected himself with his arm. Abel raised his bludgeon higher so as to bring it down on his father with even greater force.

"Abel, throw down the club!" he heard his brother shout.

Abel turned toward his father once more, to put an end to him.

"Don't!" Cain picked up a huge stone, hoisted it overhead, and hurled it. Abel crumpled to the ground.

Cain ran to his father. "Hold on to me while I remove the noose from your leg." When Adam was free, Cain attended to Abel: "Let me help you up," he said, grabbing his brother's hand.

"Let him be, son, he'll soon come to his senses," said Adam.

"He looks at me so strangely, as if the light has vanished from his eyes."

"His mind is lost. That *I* should be the ram for which he set the trap! Give him some water."

Cain unfastened the deer-belly sac that hung around his father's waist and pressed it to his brother's lips. Abel's head hung lifelessly.

"The stone you hit him with must have been too heavy, son," said Adam.

"I didn't mean to kill him."

"One who seeks his father's life does not deserve to live. But *why* did he want to kill me?"

Cain turned to his father with a deep sigh.

"It's a long story, and it would be difficult for me to repeat his bitter words."

"He attacked me with murderous rage."

"That rage may have been a sign of his cruel livelihood, Father. He insisted he had to subjugate the prime rams in order to protect the ewes. We all heard the bitter bleating of his tortured animals longing for freedom."

"Our grief at his death is unsuited for accusations," said Adam. "I could wonder at you, too, for keeping silent about his intentions."

"Would you have believed the unbelievable?"

Adam broke off a flowering branch with which to hide Abel's body from the scavenging birds.

"I shall stand guard over my brother," said Cain, taking the branch from his father's hand. "Let's not cover him just yet. Eve has the right to see her beloved son's body at rest—even if she is the cause of it all."

"Eve?"

"Doesn't the young ram go after the guardian of the flock in order to possess the ewe?" said Cain.

"But Abel was barely past childhood!"

"He perceived his coming-of-age as a man to be blocked at every turn. That's why he made an attempt on your life—how else could he have gotten to Eve?"

"You knew this? Is that why you followed me—to save my life?"

"Let's not spend more time talking, Father! It won't bring back your son. Hurry to Eve! We can't keep what has happened secret."

"I'm going, and I shall return before our Lord catches wind of Abel's death and unleashes His fury on you." Adam hurried off.

"I didn't want to kill you," murmured Cain, leaning over Abel. "Look at me and see how moved I am by your benign face. Every trace of your heartless work has disappeared from it."

The slack face of the youth who treated his sheep so harshly and sought to snuff out the life of his father was indeed transformed, and now evoked the playful years of the brothers' childhood. "I know you wouldn't have attacked our father if there had been another way for you to find a woman for yourself," said Cain. "Had I only been born a girl—I wouldn't have rejected your advances."

Cain's gaze moved beyond Abel to the far distance. Attempting to understand what had just happened, his thoughts were far from peaceful: "You can never again stand in the way of my path to Eve. Did such a motive lend a secret impetus to the movement of my hand? No! Killing you was never what I wanted. Why did you go after our father? Why didn't you kill me instead? After all that has happened, why should I live? Even if Adam were to continue to allow me to be with his woman at times, what good would it have done me? As the killer of your favorite son, I couldn't stand before you, Eve! How could I, having ended the life of the one you loved, the way you loved me before he came between us."

"I didn't want to kill you," he muttered, falling silent as he was overcome by sleep.

TWO

ADAM USUALLY PICKED up his pace when he neared his cave, but now he struggled, stopping here and there along the way. How was he going to tell his woman that one of their sons had killed the other?

He had decided to begin with "Cain saved my life!" when Eve, noticing his wounded left arm from afar, cried, "Adam, what wild beast has mauled you?"

"Abel attacked me, like a young ram who betters an ewe," Adam said, trying to steady his voice, still shaky with rage.

"Where is Abel?"

"Cain saved my life as I struggled helplessly in Abel's trap."

"And Abel?"

"Cain only wanted to thwart him, but he picked up too heavy a stone."

"I don't understand. *Where is Abel?*"

"He would have felled me with a deadly second blow of the club he had already used to injure the arm I raised to protect my head. He paid for it with his life," said Adam.

"I understand your words, Adam, but I am numb."

"If you would turn to our Lord, Eve…"

"Hold me, Adam."

"I need your womanly comfort, but I trust that our Lord will hear us and lessen our pain."

"It's easy for you, Adam; our Lord listens to you. He avoids me now that He doesn't know what to make of my womanliness."

"Talk to Him! Our Lord always says He hears our voice no matter where we are."

Eve raised her voice: "My broken heart speaks to You, O Lord. Why did You allow my son to die at the hands of my other son? You promised us that a great nation would spring from their loins!"

Eve fell silent, but, as no reply came, she spoke again with increasing bitterness: "You who know all things, did You not notice what I saw: Abel drifting onto the wrong path in his shepherding? He tamed his sheep with increasing harshness. I did nothing because I believed that everything happens according to Your plan, O Lord. We would have been more careful with our every step, our every uttered word, were it not for this foolish belief guiding us."

"Don't doubt our Creator's teaching!" cautioned Adam, afraid of their Lord's anger in the Outerworld beyond the gate of Eden. But his woman's reproachful complaints continued.

"Let Abel's death be forever an example: we can't count on our Lord's protective providence. Admit it, Lord! Declare it now and forever that You will not restrain the killing hand! Or did my son have to die simply to bring this to our consciousness? If that was Your intent, say it openly: You have no power to curb evil! Because, if we don't hear this from You, generations to come may delude themselves that they can count on Your protection."

Seeing the dread in her man's gaze, Eve's tone turned to supplication. "O Lord, I ask that You listen to this mother who grew up without a mother, who can't know if a mother is able to survive such a blow. How long can a body remain alive if the one who was ripped out of it is dead?"

Eve then tried a different way to cajole the Lord of the Garden to speak. "We thank You, O Lord, that in our vulnerable childhood You looked after us. We understand if You no longer assume that role; as adults, we shouldn't expect it of You. But if You truly are omniscient in everything that may come to pass, why didn't You teach us to avoid evil, even if You can't prevent it? And if it's truly not within Your power to curb evil, don't cause every generation of my offspring to learn it through such bitterness as we now endure! Don't give me daughters if our female descendants will give birth to siblings who will perish at each other's hand!"

Eve fixed her gaze upon the large cliff at the peak of Signal Mountain, which symbolized the Lord's Divine

Providence. When he led them out of the Garden, he told them: "If, for whatever reason, you need me, go to the peak of the highest mountain in your Outerworld and set a fire on its highest cliff. Burn fruit-bearing branches or the flesh of animals such that I may see the smoke reaching the sky from any corner of my Garden. If you call me thus, I will be with you."

At the sound of her words Eve felt again the fear and agony that overcame her before the birth of her first child. Feeling helpless, Adam set off in the direction of Signal Mountain. Upon reaching it, he kindled an enormous blaze.

"Our Lord will soon be here to help you." Adam tried to comfort his woman as soon as he returned from the mountain.

"It would help if He removed this cruel curse from me," Eve groaned in the midst of increasingly frequent contractions. Despite her great dejection she was hardly surprised their Lord stayed away. She had reason to believe that Eden's omniscient Lord knew nothing of woman's affairs, which, for the most part, filled Him with disgust.

Adam sank to his knees beside his woman, holding her hand. His touch brought a vague but unmistakable recollection: she saw herself, little Eve on her mother's bosom, two gentle hands holding her own as she pressed her fists into her mother's soft breasts.

"I too was given birth to by a mother!" Eve suddenly realized. "And my child will come out of me, somehow. Your curse to alarm me was in vain, my Lord! I will give life again and again, no matter how much pain You inflict on me. For a mother, the death of her child causes far greater pain than giving birth!"

Adam had been talking to her for some time before Eve, ruminating on the past, realized he was asking her a question.

"What might have become of us in the Garden without our Lord's Providence?"

"We were children, Adam, children!" replied Eve crossly. She would have preferred to continue brooding on the past.

"Our Lord never said He would withdraw His merciful hand from us once we grew up," Adam replied. "Not even when He cursed us and condemned us to hard work."

"Perhaps He wanted us to realize that once we're grown up we have to assume responsibility for our actions and live with the consequences of our failures."

"Are you blaming me, Eve? Is it my fault that Abel set a trap for me? That's what I'm hearing in your words."

"The problem isn't what you're hearing but what you don't want to hear. Understand once and for all: I blame our Lord because He led us to believe that everything happens with His knowledge and according to His plan. He had to know how cruel what He called 'shepherding' would make our child. The word seemed so innocent!"

"Our Lord, through what happened, must be trying to teach us that we have to take care of each other."

"But how, Adam? After all, we don't know what direction each of us must take. We can't see into each other's thoughts. We can't see the future."

"You're not trying to say, Eve, that our Lord instigated Abel's actions?"

"It's possible, Adam, that your Lord considered you too kindhearted and gentle to enact His desire for man's subjugation of woman. This is why it may have been part of His plan that Abel, who tamed his sheep with his stone-tipped club, should have dominion over me."

"What makes you think such a thing?"

"Have you forgotten how miserable your Lord made our initial years here in the Outerworld because of His curse that placed you above me?"

"It's true that we often quarreled. But we always loved each other."

"Perhaps He recognized that our love was victorious over the power of His curse."

"Or perhaps you're once again condemning Him for creating only one woman to be company for three men?"

"You too must face up to your Lord, Adam. If He foresees everything, why was He so enraged when He realized we had eaten of the fruit of the forbidden tree? And why did He create me such that I gave life to sons for whom there is no other woman? If only I could split myself in three so that each of you would have his own Eve! I saw that my firstborn was mad with unrequited desire, which we had already recognized in ourselves in the Garden and didn't know what to do about. I did what was needed to save him."

"You allowed Cain to … ?"

"What else could I do? It's possible our Lord created us according to a grand design. The world our progeny and their offspring will bring about may turn out to be wonderful—a community of love. However, until that time, we may have to endure untold misery."

"It's not our task to know why our Lord does what He does. I should go and hide Abel's body before the wild animals find him."

"Protect our remaining son as well. Take your pointed maul with you, the one you can use with one hand. I can't go to Cain after what we've just discussed. You wouldn't know whether I drew my firstborn to my breasts for comfort as his mother or as his woman, and perhaps neither would I. Go, so I can weep."

THREE

ADAM DIDN'T ROUSE his sleeping son. As he covered Abel's body with branches, he sensed the approach of the Lord of the Garden. As always, since the banishment, he was filled with cautious trepidation, even though he had done nothing wrong.

"I can't let Him harm the one who saved my life," he thought, echoing Eve's words. He didn't ask himself why he was gripping the handle of his maul as he hid himself in the underbrush.

The Lord of the Garden soon appeared, an imposing figure with long white hair and a beard that seemed to dissolve into his white robe. He watched Cain sleeping without a word. He understood full well the consequences of what had happened, as he envisioned the fulfillment of his plan not in the actions of the peace-loving Cain but in Abel's grab for power as forefather of the Outerworld's male domination. Now Abel was dead, and the anger the Lord felt toward Abel's killer prompted grave thoughts in Him.

"I could kill the sleeping fratricide brother as a deterrent to those who in the future would interfere with my plans. But dare I summon Adam, who is hiding here, and test his great strength against mine? If only I could know what it feels like to be a father, to know my wards as my own seed! Shall I provoke Adam? Shall I raise my hand against his one remaining son? Would Adam come to his son's defense? Would he attack me? He almost tried that once before when defending Eve. If only I could understand the force that binds them together, this love and desire they talk about, which seems able to make them do anything!"

The Lord rested his gaze on the sleeping Cain. Seeing him begin to stir, he raised his voice: "Where is your father's son?"

Cain started, fully awake. "I had to stop Abel, to save my father's life. I didn't mean to kill him." After a short pause he added, "What else could I have done? You didn't stop him."

The Lord of the Garden was surprised that the youth, barely grown to adulthood, dared to voice such an accusative question. He looked intently at Cain, who was emboldened by the Lord's silence.

"You said not long ago that You didn't make me the guardian of my father's son. You didn't even listen when I came to You to voice my concerns, even though You could have steered Abel, who had become increasingly cruel, onto the proper path. But You favored my younger brother's warriorlike harshness; he could tame the wildest ram through the strength of his will. Would You really have populated our world with his progeny? Is that why You turned away from me, a gentle farmer? You dismissed the crops I brought You as if they were nothing, only favoring the ewe from Abel's unhappy flock."

Adam listened in fear and wonder to the strident voice of his firstborn, who was usually prone to reticence. He knew that sooner or later their Lord's anger would strike. He crept closer.

"Why is it always a secret when and why You interfere in our lives?" he heard his son ask. "You punished my parents for their curiosity, yet that's what moves us forward. You allowed Abel to torture his enslaved rams to death, even though they're also Your creation."

The Lord roared: "Now may you be cursed on this earth which opened its mouth to receive the blood of your father's son at your hands! When you are working the soil, let it no longer give you its nourishing power. Let it produce thorns and burrs. May you eat the grass of the fields!"

"You've already hurled this curse at my father's head," Cain replied. "Yet, as a result of our diligent work, this earth has brought forth a rich harvest year after year. Take my life for the life of my younger brother, but don't threaten me with tireless work! I've heard enough from my parents about the boredom of Your Garden."

When the Lord gave no sign, Cain quoted the curse cast over Adam that he had heard from his parents: "May you earn your bread by the sweat of your brow until you return to the earth, because it is from whence you came. Dust thou art and unto dust shall thou return."

Turning into earth sounded hopeful to Cain the farmer. He realized he could never return to Eve. If she couldn't be his woman, from whose body his seed would come to life, perhaps his life would continue in the dust of the earth. He was prepared to follow his younger brother into death; he would have considered such punishment just. Nevertheless, he listened to the judgment meted out to him now with trepidation.

"May you be forever a wanderer on Earth!" the Lord proclaimed, turning away from Cain as if the matter was closed. But Cain loudly objected: "This punishment is greater than I can bear! Where can I go from here? Must I hide until the last day of my life? If anyone recognizes me as a murderer, they will surely kill me."

The Lord looked at young Cain and considered his situation. "It's worth giving this brave child a chance," he thought, motioning to Cain to come closer. "He may be of use to me as my supporter in the coming world of male domination; and if I give him some hope, he may even thrive in his exile."

"Always stand up for yourself this courageously and draw strength from the sign I will place on your forehead for your protection. Let all know: whoever would kill Cain will be punished sevenfold." Having spoken thus the Lord of the Garden stepped to a nearby bush, crumbled its crimson fruit in his hand, and, pressing a round mark with his thumb on Cain's forehead, addressed him with the following words: "Come to the shores of Gihon at sunset so I can lead you across its shallows, guarded by cherubs, and bid you on your way from my island."

Cain bowed deeply, raised the Lord's hand to his forehead, and stood in silence as Adam emerged from the forest.

"You stood up for yourself well, my son," he said, embracing his firstborn. "You will be very much missed. But our Lord is right: you can't stay here without a woman of your own. Perhaps Eve would embrace you, even after all that has happened; I would allow you to go to her, but believe me, it's not the same as sharing your life with one woman. Go and find yourself a mate!"

"But where am I to find one? After all, our Lord always said the two of you were His only human creations."

"It's true, He always said so. But when we were little He would tell us stories at night about past worlds in which speaking beings similar to us lived. Sometimes He all but admitted that He too had lived among such creatures. Of course, He liked to suggest that He has existed and will exist forever, but, between us, I have my doubts—He has grown considerably older since we've known Him, and has become more forgetful.

"I don't know if He remembered just now that after we ate of the fruit of the forbidden tree He cast the same curse over my head that He has now cast over yours. If not, you certainly reminded Him vigorously. Perhaps it's owing to this that you didn't receive a more serious punishment. Our Lord even took you under His protection."

"I wish I knew what this red spot means that He painted on my forehead with crowberry juice."

"When we were still living in the Garden, sometimes our Lord would disappear for a few days with the amber stones we gathered for Him. Then He returned with new robes and all sorts of spices, and He always wore a red spot such as this on His forehead. Trust in our Lord that He placed the sign on you to protect you from danger on your path."

"He didn't even say what direction I should go in."

"You should certainly set out toward sunrise from His island. As to where and to what end, only He knows. One thing you should pay great attention to: choose a guiding star for yourself. Get your bearings accordingly each nightfall. The greatest danger in unknown territory is walking in circles and coming across your own footprints. And don't forget: we await your return, son, if, in another world, you find a woman who suits you."

FOUR

CAIN ENCOUNTERED NUMEROUS animals as he headed toward sunrise for days on end. They watched him curiously. At first, he found their scrutiny disturbing; he assumed they knew that he had killed his own brother. He called out to them: "Aren't you bored with staring at me, you rabbit-hunting foxes and leopards? Who brought you the news of Abel's death if not the birds in the sky? I'm not afraid of the beasts of the wild as long as I have the mark of the Lord on my forehead!" He attributed their curiosity to never having seen a human being. He felt dejected by this realization, but he appreciated that they didn't bare their teeth, nor did he have to raise his walking staff to keep them at bay. This he attributed to his Lord's providence, to the protective power of the red mark he wore on his forehead.

Encouraged by the gentleness of the animals, he started talking to them, but none answered. For the most part they turned away from him, mystified. Only one small creature followed him with heightened interest, venturing ever closer. Whenever the wanderer stopped and looked back at his stalker it sat down and, turning its head aside, made as if something else had captured its attention. After the animal had played this game several times, Cain settled down on a suitable rock in the cool air of daybreak and started to eat the berries and seeds he had gathered. Seeing the food, it was not just curiosity that overcame the animal's shyness. It came closer as Cain threw fat seeds toward it. Cain saw that it had hairy hands rather than hoofs, goat nails, or tiger claws; it was as if they were human hands, the size of baby Abel's when he could barely squeeze his big brother's finger.

"Is it childhood that makes you so small?" Cain softly asked, so as not to scare it away. "Will you grow up into an Eve?" The way it turned its head this way and that suggested it understood something of what the giant addressing it said.

Cain, starved for a human voice and closeness, tried again to make himself understood, but to no avail. Perhaps it is too young, he thought, still hopeful. But that hope dissipated once the creature enticed others like it into the clearing that encircled the tamarisk tree. None were bigger than the one Cain had somewhat befriended, not even the one who approached him holding its baby pressed against its breast with half an arm, jumping toward him on three legs, more slowly than the others.

He watched the extended family with envy as they settled next to him, its members beginning to groom one another with devoted attention. Having found no potential mate among them, however, he eventually bid them farewell.

He continued to think out loud to cheer himself on. "Lord, why did You send me on my way into this world? To find an Eve? Why did You allow me to live if You give no purpose to my life? Should I have lied to You? Should I have said that I was jealous of Abel and his large flock and that's why I felled him?

"Would You have struck me down with Your bolt of lightning to extinguish my suffering? Or did You banish me because, by killing my brother, I thwarted You from seeing the spectacle of Abel in his yearning for a woman beating the rams bloody for defending the ewes from his advances? Did You create my parents only so You could put them to the test at every turn and take pleasure in their suffering? I know You loved my mother and father as Your own children when they were young, but why did You abandon them when they began to question You? How did You dare to create Eve if, when she turned to You with uncertainties about becoming a woman, Your knowledge extended merely to telling stories of the Garden's trees and animals?

"You say nothing? No matter. I'm talking aloud only to keep hope alive that my voice may carry to someone who understands my words. Perhaps You will cast another curse over me. You, yes, *You* killed Abel by pitting him against his father! Why do You allow Abel to stand before me in the dark each night? Why? Do the dead, instilling fear in the living, give life purpose?

"Do you appear before me each night, my little brother, so my fear convinces me that I have transgressed against you? Is this how you would delude yourself that you are innocent? Enough! I won't allow you to ruin my life!"

Cain wondered: "Is it possible that my brother appears in my dreams to warn me of some danger stemming from not having listened to him before he attacked our father? Why am I afraid to relive the day when Abel shared his plans with me? Is this why I wake up alarmed from my dreams whenever I hear the bitter bleating of his rams? Am I afraid that I will become the ram if I allow my dreams to continue? Could the past have been altered, if I told Adam what his younger son was plotting against him? Perhaps this is what I must understand."

The wanderer lay down beneath a tree's shelter from the fire of the sun and let himself be lulled into dreams. Although he soon heard a ram's desperate bleating, it didn't wake him with a start the way it had many nights before. He saw himself planting seeds in the rich soil of the field beside the brook in the Outerworld. Abel ran toward him.

"That beast got away. Did you see it?" asked Abel, panting, exactly as he had done on the day he attacked Adam.

"I hope you never catch up to it. Its skin hung in shreds—it's a wonder it could still move, with its back broken," Cain heard his own voice, then Abel's again: "Shut up, or you'll get yours too!" Abel raised his club, crimson from the ram's blood. "Why do you stand with him against me? I just want to frighten off the rams that come to protect their ewes. One of them recently lurched at the walls of the pen to free my women."

"Your women? You were serious the other day, when you said it's better with a ewe than nothing? Have you lost your mind, Abel?"

"It's easy for you to rant. I know Eve lets you be with her sometimes. Don't deny it! I saw you."

Cain was surprised: he didn't remember those words in his waking state or his reply.

"You're peeping too? The things you're capable of!" In his dream, Cain bent to plant another seed. Abel kicked him in the rear and he fell forward on his face. Cain jumped at his brother, grabbing him by the waist. He held him tight to restrain him, remembering their wrestling as children—the tight embraces from which he didn't always want to pull away. In the dream, however, he understood their wrestling as the last time they tested their strength against each other. Abel was the one to give up. "I can't overpower you yet, but you can see I'm no longer a child. I have as much right to Eve as you. Our Lord didn't create a separate woman for each of us. And that's exactly what I want to talk with you about, Cain. I learned long ago that two rams in one pen don't fit. The younger ram, in time, overpowers the dominant one, so he can get to his ewes."

"You're not thinking of yourself and Adam? He's your father and twice as strong as you are!"

"The two of us together could overcome him."

Cain was shocked by Abel's words. "Even so, there would be two of us remaining," he replied, which he hadn't recalled until his dream. Had it appeared to his brother that he accepted the alliance against their father? Perhaps Abel detailed his plan further for that reason.

"One of us could get this Outerworld that our Lord bequeathed to Adam when He banished them from His Garden."

"And the other?"

"The other, Eve." Abel came forward at last with what he thought to be a compelling argument.

"Don't you think Eve would have a say in this?"

"But she lets you come to her!"

"That's different…"

"Why is it different?"

Cain remembered how wise he felt his reply was: "Her love for you as her son is more than it is for me. That's why she won't let you near her."

"What kind of nonsense is that?" asked Abel, not comprehending.

"When I was born, Eve didn't know what to do with me, having grown up without a mother. She took me to her breasts not only to feed me. But we can't be judgmental; after all, what could she have known about motherhood? Nor did the Lord of the Garden create a female sibling for her with whom she could talk over her feelings."

"But I still don't understand why I wouldn't be as good for Eve as you, if she would let me close."

"That's not the point…"

"What, then?"

"Let's sit down. What I want to say is about both of us. After you came out of my mother's body, I realized that I also came into the world that way. Then my mother took you instead of me to her breast, and I cried bitterly, and stamped my feet, until, sometimes, she would take me to her. I started to recall that she took me to her bosom sometimes even when I wasn't hungry. Then she would play with me in other ways."

"You're lying."

"I also remember that, in those days, she wouldn't allow Adam to come near our cave. She had him put the food he brought in the morning on a faraway rock. I only began to understand why when they started arguing more often."

"Adam is much stronger. Why did he allow Eve…"

"You won't understand while you continue to seek companionship in your sheep. There are powers other than the strength you feel in your arms, Abel."

"We have to join forces. Then we can share Eve."

"What do you imagine me to be?" Cain heard himself say, and felt in his dream the outrage he experienced when this conversation had taken place. "You must take a look at yourself, brother. If I were to tell our father..."

"You ass! Why didn't our mother give birth to a girl for my growing desire instead of you? Or do you think I'll be satisfied with bleating sheep forever? Know this, Cain: our Lord can only count on me to carry out His plan through my indefatigable will. I will enact male dominion above all else."

Cain heard Abel's words in his dream, but they were not spoken in reality. Neither was what his brother shouted as he left, enraged: "Well, if this is what you want, let us be at war!"

At this, Cain awoke and looked around, frightened. He saw the sunny landscape, which seemed more peaceful than on any other day of his journey, and he was reassured.

"Yes, this is what happened before Abel struck our father," he said to himself, reflecting on his dream. "I had to see once more every line of his face, hear every unspoken word, and understand every ulterior thought. And I?

Could I have done otherwise than I did? Could I have made my ambitious brother come to peace with his destiny? Better that I move on now so I can keep the scorching sun behind me."

He started off, but his thoughts continued: "Should I have told my father what his younger son planned? Adam might have thought that I, too, was plotting against him. But I was wrong to have remained silent, even if I always accompanied my father through the fields and forests. I never took my watchful eyes off him. Should I have known that I could only protect my father's life at the cost of Abel's? Or did I calculate that, standing on our father's side, I could be free of my younger brother? If we win another's forgiveness what good is it, if we can't forgive ourselves? This is what penance must be for: the long and bitter road on which our Lord has sent us.

"I now admit I needed every step of this journey to be free of doubt and self-recrimination that I saved my father's life at the cost of my brother's. I heard Abel's words spoken while he was still alive in my dream, but why do I still feel that he wishes to speak to me? Is it perhaps because he sees the past differently from the land of the dead? Speak to me, Abel! Say that you forgive me! That one word would redeem me from further penance."

The wanderer sat down in the shade of a tree. He cast off his thoughts so as to make way for Abel's. The sun had nearly completed its daily passage in the sky when he heard his younger brother's voice at last.

"You will not hear the word 'forgiveness' from me, because there is nothing for me to forgive. You did not take my life; in that world into which I was born, I had no life. Now that I live inside you and see Eve through your eyes I know that, even if I could have overpowered both you and my father, she would never have been mine. Her will is greater than ours. I couldn't believe this at the time, but now I know it is as you said: 'There are greater forces, Abel, than the power you feel in your arms!' Do you know, my brother, what the force that dwells in Eve is? Her power is the knowledge that she, Eve, is the Giver of Life. We men can take life but we cannot give it. You could only save our father's life if you killed me. Live instead of me, Cain! You will gain my forgiveness if you remember me not as the envious, hateful person you saw me to be in the final years of my life. Think of me as a child, when I looked up to you with adoration."

Upon hearing these words, Cain rose up. He had been forgiven, and he now had sufficient strength and conviction to continue on his journey, despite the falling darkness.

The next day, the wanderer's heart nearly stopped beating as he found human footprints in the sand. He became fearful, believing they might be his own, no matter how careful he had always been to start out at dawn each day toward the rising sun. Engrossed in his thoughts, perhaps he had, after all, walked in a circle? But when he looked behind him he saw that the unknown footprints crossed his own path. He stepped into the footprint in front of his, and found it was smaller than his own. It could be Eve's, he thought joyfully. But then he detected another, bigger footprint.

"Adam and Eve?" he asked himself. "Am I to be third here too?" Bitterness filled him. "What should I do now? Follow my path according to the direction of sunrise as designated by our Lord or follow these footprints?"

Cain peered into the distance. Something green was apparent where the sand vanished into nothingness.

"If those are trees or bushes, there must be water as well." He patted his flattened flask. "I'll go that far. After all, I do need water, and I may find people."

He did as he had decided, but as soon as he came closer to the trees he saw that the footprints avoided the little oasis, and he quickly learned why. Whitened animal skeletons lay scattered in the sand. There were more among the trees. Next to the stones surrounding a well-marked watering hole lay something he had never seen before but immediately recognized—a human skeleton. The open-mouthed skull gaped, as if to warn passersby not to drink from the well's water.

"I must get to clean water today, tomorrow at the latest," thought Cain. "Those who avoided this place must know where they can quench their thirst. It's best if I follow their footsteps."

This is how it came to be that Cain reached the crest of a low mountain range. He could hardly believe his eyes. Below him, so close he could have shouted out to them, were people! Throughout his journey, he had imagined that he might meet another human being. But seeing so many at the same time filled him with trepidation.

"Could they be expecting me? Did our Lord let them know to wait here for the one who killed his brother? How many Abels can there be among so many humans? If there are Eves among them, how can I find mine? And how many Abels must I fight for her?"

A huge weight settled on Cain's chest. "Are they also in exile?" he wondered. "Could our Lord have sent me into a world of evil outlaws? If He knew of the existence of this world, why did He lead us to believe that there were no other human creations on Earth?"

In the depths of his soul he sensed that his entire world, all that he held to be true until now, all that he believed, would collapse if he found an answer to this last question.

AND CAIN WENT OUT
FROM THE PRESENCE
OF THE LORD, AND DWELT
IN THE LAND OF NÓD
ON THE EAST OF EDEN.
AND CAIN KNEW HIS WIFE;
AND SHE CONCEIVED,
AND BARE ENOCH:
AND HE BUILDETH
A CITY, AND CALLED
THE NAME OF THE CITY
AFTER THE NAME OF
HIS SON, ENOCH.

GENESIS 4:16-17

II

Cain in the Land *of* Nód

FIVE

CAIN BROKE OUT in a sweat. He noticed that the people standing just two stone throws away were holding sharply pointed spears that appeared more lethal than his brother's club. He saw innumerable tiny figures in the crevice of the valley. Some disappeared, as if the earth had swallowed them, while others came forth from roundish mounds of earth. These were not ants, however; *humans* milled about.

Throughout his long journey as a wanderer, the hope that, in addition to Adam's Eve, there might be another female being in existence somewhere had kept him alive. Now, as he viewed so many people, he felt inhibited. His fright subsided somewhat, however, when he saw that those closer to him were digging holes to plant seeds in the ground with their dangerous spearlike implements, just as he had done in his parents' Outerworld. They were also using a sharpened rock with no handle. "They are clever," he thought. "It's easier this way. I can learn from them. They're not using their spears as weapons. Why am I afraid of them—simply because they are so numerous? I should call out to them, but what shall I say so they welcome me with open hearts?"

Meanwhile, the people set down their work, took up their bundles and jugs, and together started down the mountain. The last in line, an elderly man, wore a white robe almost to the ground, just like the Lord of the Garden. The garb of the others was resplendent in a myriad of colors and covered their chests but didn't reach their knees. The light fabric barely concealed the handsome contours of their bodies.

"Look, there are some Eves among them!" a voice shouted within him. "But there are so many! What if they turn against me?"

Cain tried to yell but no sound came from his throat. Then the devastation of being alone that had accompanied him on his seemingly endless pilgrimage overcame his momentary paralysis, and he cried out in a voice more like a wounded beast's rasping howl:

"I am human too!"

His words brought the procession to a halt. They looked at each other, bewildered. The white-robed man cast his glance back and forth, trying to discover who belonged to the voice coming from the bushes.

"Who is it that claims to be human?" he asked.

Cain could barely stand upright on his quaking legs

but, taking hold of himself, he stepped out from his hiding place.

"I see that in fact you are human. But where did you come from?" asked the ramrod-straight old man, moving closer to take better stock of Cain, whose hair and beard were gray with the dust of travel, his face blackened with muddy sweat. Having received no reply, the old man turned to his companions: "He must be a wild man from the forest. Look down into the valley lest his companions attack us."

"Do you have any other words?" a woman gently asked Cain.

"Maybe he's a headhunter," speculated a yellow-robed youth. "My grandfather told me he almost lost his head once upon encountering such unwashed wild men who wore similar fur wraparounds, strapped at the shoulder."

"But he doesn't even have a spear!"

"Let's get away from here. I can't stand his stench."

"Maybe he isn't so old after all. The mud from his journey is deepening his wrinkles."

"And his bearing isn't bent."

"Tell us at least where you come from," asked a woman who looked to be the oldest of three curious companions.

Cain was unable to speak this time because he was so stunned that all these female humans looked different from one another, since the Eves his desire conjured up daily all looked exactly like his father's woman.

"If every Eve is different, how can I know which should be mine? Will she accept me, as I am considered to be, according to the boisterous voices raised just now, not only a headhunter but mentally deranged, or perhaps even a spy?"

More hostile grumblings erupted when someone commented: "He may be one of those nomads who poisoned the wells lying toward the setting sun." Someone even suggested that at most only this dog-voiced upstart's mother might have been human. They tried to guess within earshot of Cain what kind of animal his father might have been.

Cain could not abide this affront. He cleared his throat to speak when the white-robed man stepped forward. "My name is Kihara-gyó," he said, emphasizing the "gyó." "But you can call me simply Kihara. What are you afraid of, son? Everyone knows that we people of Nód never harm a sojourner who has good intentions. What is that mark on your forehead?"

"Perhaps it is their holy sign, only very faded," said the woman who had addressed him earlier.

"Where are you from, son?" asked Kihara-gyó again. "If your mouth is not yet ready for speech, perhaps you could point to the direction from where you came."

Cain pointed in the direction of the sunset, and with that his tongue also loosened: "I came from my father's Outerworld. The full moon rose only a few days after our

Lord bid me on my way. For all those long days I saw the rising sun before me, and I always kept the setting sun behind me."

"No wonder he looks so tired. Let's give him something to eat," said a woman, signaling her daughter, who stood beside her to offer her food bag to the newcomer. Then she added: "Although he doesn't look it, judging from his speech he comes from a good family."

"Are you perhaps from the banks of the Euphrates?" asked Kihara.

"Not from its banks but even beyond its surge. My parents, the sole human creations of our Lord, stayed in the Outerworld."

At these words so many questions descended upon Cain that he understood only a few.

"Outerworld?"

"What is this Outerworld?"

"Whose creatures are your parents?"

Cain looked at Kihara, waiting for a question he could answer.

"Where is this Outerworld that we have never heard of?"

"Beyond not only the Euphrates but on the island of the Garden of Paradise and Gihon River."

"Gihon, where is Gihon?" asked those encircling him.

"What is your name? And how did you cross over

the tides of the rivers?" These further questions came from Kihara.

"I am Cain. Our Lord led me across the shallows of the river."

"What kind of lord are you talking about? Was he perhaps the one who put this mark upon your forehead?"

"Yes, it was our Lord, who created my parents. He placed it upon my forehead for protection."

"When?"

"Before He exiled me," answered Cain, immediately regretting his words. Everyone recoiled as if he had confessed to being a leper. The clamor suddenly turned hostile.

"You were exiled?"

"What did you do?"

"He must have killed someone!"

Others consulted with Kihara, who ultimately came to a decision and spoke in a voice of official capacity.

"If you are an exile, the Dowager Council must decide if they will admit you into our peaceful city. You must go before them."

They led him toward the anthills, which, Cain understood from their words, they called a city: the city of Nód. The younger ones ran ahead to announce the mysterious foe's arrival. A boisterous crowd gathered to greet him.

Seeing the multitude, Cain was again overcome with fear. His anxiety only increased when, as he gleaned from their excited words, the messengers introduced him as the perpetrator of heinous crimes.

"What will you do with me?" he asked, trembling, but his words were lost in the cacophony of questions addressed to him. He had nearly given up all hope when, upon passing through the city, they reached a large field. The crowd dispersed so as to surround the elevation located in its center, which was occupied by five women. Stopping a few paces from them, Kihara deeply bowed, then stepped away from Cain and addressed him so loudly that even those standing afar could hear.

"Cain, you are standing before the Council of Dowager Dames. If you tell the truth in everything, your judgment will be just. We must know why you were exiled from that Outerworld of yours. The question is under what judgment your deed falls according to the laws of Nód."

Cain was ready to speak in his own defense, but Kihara waved him off.

"Do not say anything that you may regret later. Whatever leaves your lips determines how we hear and evaluate your subsequent words because we, the people of Nód, living in peace, never condemn a deed if we do not understand the reason behind it. Since I was the one to have first spoken with you, a foreigner from far away, I consider myself to be your oldest and best friend. According to our customs, therefore, I must be the one to bring your case before the Council and to the people. Later you may find someone else who stands by your side, but for now I am beside you and it is upon my soul if, because of an error on my part, an unjust sentence is passed."

After this Kihara-gyó turned to the women's Council and described the foreigner's arrival and his words with uncanny accuracy. After his summary the woman seated in the center, slightly higher than the others, introduced her companions one by one, and then herself:

"I am Mahanna-ma. I direct the Council of Grand Dames. I will pose the questions put forth by my partners. You will answer me and you may consult Kihara-gyó as your friend at any time. Do you accept?"

Cain was only able to nod.

"So, your name is Cain. Who gave you this lovely name? Your father? Your mother?"

"I was told that it was our Lord, the Lord of the Garden, who told my parents to name their firstborn thus."

"Yes, the Lord of the Garden, we shall return to that. But tell us, inasmuch as you know that Lord of the Garden, in what respect did he recommend that you be given this name?"

Cain looked at his new friend perplexed, at which point Kihara explained that the word *cain*, in Nód, meant "acquisition," "profit," or sometimes "founder." "Moreover, there was a time we even called blacksmiths 'cain,'" added Kihara after a brief pause for thought.

"I think 'founder' is most appropriate. According to my father, Adam, our Lord planned through us to establish a great nation, a world. He may have thought of it as our Outerworld."

"And how many people live in that Outerworld?" asked Mahanna.

"Only two remain now, my parents, Adam and Eve."

"And you have no siblings?"

"Abel..." Cain looked at his advocate with such despair that Kihara came to stand next to him, and they consulted at length. Cain repeated several times what had happened and why. In the end, together, they composed the shortest reply that incorporated everything that had happened.

"My brother Abel died. He died by my hand, but not of my will. I had to thwart him. He desired to possess Eve and take our father's life!"

After a few moments of stunned silence, the people cried out as one and began moving toward him. "Murderer!" and "Fratricide!" could be heard in the ominous clatter. Cain instinctively drew closer to his friend.

"Don't be afraid," Kihara said. "It will be better that you have told the worst of it this way. They will be embarrassed by their harsh outbursts and will accept with great empathy what you say in your own defense."

"It is as if they didn't even hear that my action was in defense of my father."

"We condemn violence, whatever its motivation, because we believe that our chief god, Hunán, gave us the ability to speak so we could resolve our differences with words."

"I spoke with my little brother. I tried to persuade him to see things in a better light. But talk was in vain."

"Do not underestimate the power of speech! If you wish for the people of Nód to accept you into their fold, do not build your defense on this, because we do not take kindly to those who are unable to disarm others with words. If you truly acted in defense of your father, the question is, how can you prove it? You must do only one thing for now: tell the truth to the Grand Dame in everything lest you become entangled in lies from which you cannot unravel yourself."

"I will tell the truth in everything, because I will perish if you too exile me," promised the newcomer.

Throughout all this Mahanna conferred with her women companions, then signaled the multitude to be quiet so she could pose the following question to Cain: "In your beleaguered condition we cannot ascertain your age. Tell us, how many seasons have you lived?"

"According to my father I completed my fourteenth rainy season this year and am now in my fifteenth summer."

"And the one you call your Lord, did he educate you in your youth?"

"In my youth, yes. But after I started walking the forests and fields with my father I could not abide sitting at the foot of our Lord for even half a day. My mother also thought it better if I avoided Him, as He made her life difficult."

"Why difficult? Did your mother say?"

"When He exiled them from His Garden, our Lord ordered her to be under her husband's dominion, but…" Cain wanted to list other reasons, but the word "Matúzs" resounded from the crowd.

Mahanna conferred with the women and addressed Cain.

"You must have heard the people mention Matúzs. What you said about your Lord's curse demeaning Eve by placing her beneath Adam reminds us of someone who in our youth brought troubled times upon us, almost defiling our peaceful existence here in Nód.

"According to our custom we are not allowed to adjourn your hearing until we have given you every opportunity to clear yourself. But with good reason we also presume that you may be able to help us with an important matter that has preoccupied us for a generation, son."

Cain was much comforted by this friendly address. Nevertheless, he looked questioningly at Kihara, who hurried over to the women, as did another, slightly younger man. They conferred at length, after which Mahanna introduced the other man.

"This is Kio-gyó, our beloved storyteller and teaching master. He maintains that he is in possession of such knowledge as can help you understand yourself and help us in admitting you. Of course, we know that you would like to be done with this hearing, but Kio-gyó, who would also like to be by your side, asked us to give him a day to gather his thoughts. Your words shed light on many things for him but also led him to serious new questions. Let us all, therefore, meet here tomorrow when Kio is ready to take his place on the storytelling rock. You, Cain, remain under the protection of your friend Kihara, who will guide you around our city and tell you the story of long ago that Kió wishes to speak about tomorrow."

SIX

"COME WITH ME, son," Kihara signaled to Cain. "Let's eat something, and then I will show you our city."

Cain was concerned that the crowd, which earlier had frightened him so, would surround him again. But people had already dispersed into their houses, as if the earth had swallowed them up. Cain thought what they called houses were entrances to caves beneath the earth.

"Tell me, did you live with your parents in a house similar to this in the Outerworld?" Kihara asked when they stopped in front of a house under construction. It had a rounded roof and a square foundation made of braided stalks held together with clay.

"Abel pitched a tent for himself from branches and hides when he started living with his sheep. We, on the other hand, could choose from numerous caves," the newcomer answered.

As they proceeded toward the center of the city, a colorfully vibrant building, perhaps ten times larger than the ones he had just seen, captured his attention.

"That, my son, is the house of holy Hunán," Kihara proudly explained. "We worship many gods, as I assume you do too, but above them all stands Hunán, invisible to the human eye, inscrutable to the mind. For you, does the Lord of the Garden stand above all other gods?"

"According to my father, the Lord created them from the dust of the earth and watches over them."

"And do you believe and trust in his Providence?"

"Not so much, perhaps. I have often hoped that He would fulfill my only wish, but to no avail. Now that I have come upon your world of many Eves, I hope He sent me to you because He knew you would accept me and I would find my own Eve here. Yet, He puts my faith to the test over and over again, as is apparent from the outcry of many here against me."

"The multitude is like fallen leaves in autumn–every breeze rustles it. Your unexpected appearance from this mysterious Outerworld, neither seen nor heard of, and your exile from there has stirred up our people like a whirlwind. I will get an important ally for you from Hunán's temple. I will ask its priestess Cikara to come to Kio's storytelling act of confession tomorrow. We may need her wise counsel."

Cain started to follow him toward the temple, but Kihara held him back.

"You may not enter here until you wash off the mud

from your journey. Stay here undisturbed with these nice merchant women." He led his protégé to the open market. "I will return soon."

The newcomer was once again surrounded by people whose curiosity was heightened by what they had heard from or about him. Cain felt the few moments his friend left him by himself to be an eternity, especially when he encountered more than friendly curiosity. Four youths started a conversation with him, then called him aside and rebuked him.

"We can't admit such a foul-smelling human into Nód," said one, turning away in disgust.

Cain started to recount the hardships of his long pilgrimage, but they responded to his words with derision. They next charged him with espionage and poisoning wells, shoving him roughly. He was about to raise his fist when some of the merchants came to his aid.

"Don't hit them, Cain!" interceded one of the merchant women. "That's exactly what they want; an excuse not to accept you among us. We know these hooligans."

"Get lost, you miserable loafers!" a butcher, holding a cleaver, yelled at the assailants, who fled.

Cain eventually calmed down enough to speak: "Kihara, who stood by my side in front of the women, said you are a peaceful people."

"There are hot-tempered youths everywhere," commented the butcher.

"As well as hostile, racist older people," added a market woman at her herb stand. Cain surmised she was from a faraway land; she differed from the others in her language and dress.

"I'll get Kihara-gyó—the Grand Dames entrusted him with Cain's protection," said a man, entering the temple.

An angry Kihara arrived and immediately took his upset protégé to his house. He ladled rainwater into a tub so Cain could cleanse himself from his journey. The newcomer had to ask for fresh water four times before he felt he was ready to sit down to supper.

After they had eaten, Kihara asked Cain to sit at his feet. "I will tell you what everyone here knows so you can understand what Kió will be recounting. First of all, many other worlds exist outside and beyond here, and many different people live in them whose language differs from ours."

"I'm glad I didn't know this," remarked Cain. "What always spurred me on my journey was that perhaps I would come across a speaking being. I would have been bitterly disappointed if I had met an Eve whose words I didn't understand."

"Don't worry. If you are allowed to stay with us, you will surely find a woman whose every word you will understand and whose voice you will always be pleased to hear."

"But if I understand correctly, you spoke just now not only about women. Why don't you understand each other's words?"

"According to an ancient legend, a very long time ago, when people all spoke one language, they began to build a tower that turned out to be so tall the priests placed on Earth by the gods in heaven feared it would be discovered that no one lived up there at all."

"Gods living in the sky? Perhaps our Lord also came down to be among us. Was it finally resolved whether anyone lived up there?"

"No. The priests and shamans, who live on the offerings brought for their gods, confounded the people's tongues with magic. They no longer understood each other, and so they could not continue with the tower's construction. This, of course, is only a story; the way our imagination fills in the unbearable voids that stem from ignorance. We can also envision, however, that when people lived on the banks of great waters or in the valleys of high mountains they found words with which they could communicate with one another about their own world. At least this is what our own Matúzs taught us. But let me finally tell you who Matúzs is, about whom Kió wants to talk."

"Before you do that, Kihara, I would like to ask what you meant by my finding a woman whose voice I would always be pleased to hear. I ran away from my mother frequently because she always wanted to teach me. I sided with my father because, although I was never interested in hunting, we could sit next to each other in silence for much of the day. We didn't want to scare away the animals. It was only after we were successful that we told each other where we had wandered in our thoughts. When I sat in front of our cave by myself Eve always asked what I was thinking, even before my thoughts led anywhere."

"This is the way mothers are, Cain. But it is apparent from your words that we men are predominantly the offspring of hunters and are the more silent people. You cannot entice an animal to you with words, the way market women do buyers. But then, it is not the father but the mother who warbles to her infant on her bosom. You too must have learned most of your words from your mother. A silent mother will not have a richly conversant child, we say in Nód. But if you select your partner well, she will be your woman and not your mother."

Cain was happy to muse about such Eves, and Kihara saw that it would be of no use now to relate the story he had planned to tell Cain. It was based on events that had shocked everyone in their world long ago. Cain was too tired to listen, and Kihara showed him to his sleeping quarters, made comfortable with soft woven fabrics. Cain lay down upon them and slept.

In his dream, Cain felt his future Eve's head on his shoulder. It felt odd that she didn't have his mother's face. He saw her smile at their child in her lap. The warmth he felt in his heart slowly descended to his groin. And then the Eve, whose face he still didn't see, embraced the dreaming Cain.

"This is your mission," he heard in his dream. "But will the people of Nód understand what has led me to them?" He quickly dismissed this voice of doubt.

When he opened his eyes, he saw Kihara standing before him, blocking the light of the rising sun. Kihara offered him some delicious fruit, then invited his friend on a long walk. The people of Nód were mostly still sleeping, so the newcomer was able to enjoy all the beauty of the city without being disturbed. He admired the colorful pattern of inlaid stones in front of the temple.

Not far away, beneath a high roof, a man was bent in front of a huge fire shooting off sparks. Kihara introduced him as the city's best blacksmith.

"I hear you were a farmer in the Outerworld," said the blacksmith, signaling for them to come closer. "As soon as the fire takes on more of a glow I'll make you a digging tool suited to your hand, the kind that will never dull because I will not make the tip out of pure brass the way our ancestors did. We add some white ore to it, which makes it much harder." The smith allowed Cain to take a hammer. "Always hit where I have hit," the master instructed Cain. Together they pounded flat an incandescent piece of metal.

The master next went to a cluster of wooden poles leaning against the wall. "Let me see which one suits your hand." He measured a few against Cain, selected one, and returned to the fire, where he skillfully formed the tip of the wedge, glowing once again, around the end of the rod and then dipped the now flaming wood into a cistern.

"It will never fall off," said the smith. "Such a digging pole will make your work easier if you wish to continue working the soil. If not, I will take you on beside me anytime!" He patted Cain's shoulder.

"At least he accepts me," thought Cain happily, as he bid farewell to the smith.

"You will see, son, how easy it is to break the soil with this," said Kihara, making digging motions by the edge of the stone road. "But there are people not so far away from us, in the nearby cities and villages, whose masters forge weapons that cut through anything, including the heads of those their king considers their enemy." Kihara felled an imaginary enemy with the cutting edge of the spade, proving thereby how one can turn human ingenuity and dexterity toward good and evil at the same time.

"Are there populations where fratricide to some kings is a virtue?" asked Cain. "They would surely accept me," he added acerbically.

In the course of their conversation, Kihara showed so many things to his young friend that by the afternoon Cain knew more about Nód and its traditions than many natives. Everyone wanted to win over to their own craft the visitor from a distant mysterious world. Cain learned the rudiments of weaving, carving, and shaping clay dishes. He was so engrossed in all this activity that he seldom recalled the four foul youths who bullied him.

"Perhaps all the novelty I have showed you has made you tired. It is important that you see with your own eyes how we live. I still have to tell you one more thing before we meet Kió. We need to rest first; it may be a long night."

Many questions remained pent up in Cain. When Kihara went into his house, Cain found a place to lie down in the shade of the garden. He could not yet bring himself to go into the house, being as yet unable to comprehend how its roof didn't collapse. Dreams quickly swept him away.

SEVEN

KIHARA WOKE CAIN as the sun was setting. He had Cain sit at his feet and began the instruction Mahanna requested.

"Have you heard the name Matúzs in your Outerworld?" Kihara asked.

"I seem to recall hearing it from my mother's mouth when she was arguing with my father."

"I have reason to believe that we shall hear it often from Kió, so, it is best that you know that *matúzs* means 'wise old man.' When I was young there was someone living among us who, although not old by any means, nevertheless had insight into everything such that we began calling him Matúzs. We loved and respected him very much. But one day, when he returned from one of his sunrise journeys, it was as if he had lost all reason. He told stories of people who named their children not after their mother but after the supposed father. In the beginning we considered this merely laughable; although we have always liked to live in pairs, there are also instances with us when the mother doesn't even know who the father is."

"I thought every man-person had his own Eve here," interjected Cain.

Kihara smiled indulgently—he had already learned that the newcomer liked to steer every conversation toward the subject of the numerous Eves. He took a deep breath in order to be able to say as much as possible without his pupil interrupting.

"Matúzs proclaimed that the era of matriarchs was over because we humans have multiplied to such an extent that we will soon inhabit all the fertile farmland. Soon, he said, we will have to defend ourselves and our fields not only from wild beasts but from each other. Only people led by men will be able to accomplish this—trained hunters."

"Why did he say that 'we have multiplied to such as extent'? I didn't meet another human being for many days before my arrival here."

"You came from the direction of sunset, where only nomads who do not like foreigners live. Their laws, however, require them to treat those who wander into their camp as guests. As a result, they kill those heading their way before they reach their tents. They also wage battle with those who graze their animals on their unmarked fields and steal animals even if they have no need of them."

"Abel would also do anything to increase his flock, even if he had trouble managing the animals he had already broken in."

These words piqued Kihara's interest. He inquired at length about the newcomer's sibling, parents, their life in the Outerworld, and, of course, about their Lord, the Lord of the Garden. All the while he recounted many stories about Nód:

"You see, son, this is the big difference between the old order in which we live and the new male dominance that Matúzs proclaimed and whose arrival we fear. In the old order there is no ownership, no power inequality. The men hunt but do not possess beasts, and that is how it should be. The women take care of the family and thereby all families of the city."

"Are you saying that Mahanna-ma, your guardian, is Nód's ruler?" Cain asked, because he noticed that everyone paid attention to her.

"She merely gives voice to what the Grand Dames decide. It is not being ruled that we have to fear, Cain, but the lust for power. The one in power might even be benevolent were it not that the lust for power in others must be curbed, even at the price of taking their heads. On the other hand, women's alliance is based on kinship, and you can't acquire kinship by force."

At that point, Mahanna arrived at the garden and immediately took over the conversation.

"Men always covet their neighbor's field, but with women close by you can live in security, as we in Nód can affirm. Everything you told Cain is important. He must know all this if he is to stay with us. But now he must understand who Matúzs is. Have you told Cain already what happened when Matúzs was still among us?"

Kihara nodded and resumed his narrative: "Matúzs was instigating against the women with increasing fervor until the Elders came to a decision and exiled him. 'If he wishes to be in the bellicose world of male dominance, if he does not believe in the pacifying power of words, he should leave here,' was the majority opinion.

"In some of his sermons he promised great glory to the few in Nód he was able to get on his side, ready to wage battle. I must confess, for a time he was even able to captivate me, until I came to understand that his plan for male dominance would inevitably lead to ongoing wars. It could never bring about the eternal peace whose coming he preached. But before I recognized this..."

It was obvious that Kihara would have liked to excuse his previous actions, but a single impatient motion by Mahanna was enough for him to return to Matúzs.

"We were relieved when, by dawn of the day after his exile, it was proclaimed there was neither sight nor sign of him. Our happiness was short-lived, however, because we discovered that two small children had disappeared with him, a suckling infant boy and a little girl barely beyond feeding at her mother's breast. Only Matúzs could have abducted them," explained Kihara.

Cain was surprised: "You call him wise, he who kidnapped children from their parents?"

"The wisest person can be swept into insanity when he sees the future and convinces himself that only he knows the way there. Matúzs lost his mind because we didn't listen to him.

"We were terribly worried about the two children. Our people immediately started out to all corners of the earth to find them. To no avail. Ever since, we have weaved fantastic tales about their fate, from pitiful to glorious."

"Alright, Kihara. That will be enough for him to understand anything Kió might disclose," said Mahanna, standing up. "Let's hurry so we don't miss anything."

EIGHT

Nód's young and old gathered on the Big Field that night. The calls of vendors could barely be heard above the din. Kio-gyó spread fur hides on the rock called the Talking Chair to indicate that he was preparing for a long evening.

Mahanna addressed the people first: "We have always followed Kio-gyó's accounts of his travels with great interest, and today he is going to tell us something we have been wanting to hear for thirty years. He must also explain why he has kept silent about it until now. You have the floor, Kió."

"I know every word of what I want to say to be true, although you know very well that sometimes memory surpasses what is real. Mahanna mentioned that it has been nearly thirty years since the two children disappeared and several of us, including myself, set out to find them. I searched with no success. No one saw which way the kidnapper went. More than ten years after the disappearance of Matúzs and the two innocents, I started out again. I'll tell you why.

"Almost seventeen years ago I acquired an exceptionally large amber stone, said to have healing properties, from a merchant of a distant sunset city." Kió displayed a beautiful translucent stone, about the size of a dove's egg and pale yellow in color. "I placed it in my treasure chest at home and to my amazement another very similar one already sparkled there." Kió raised another amber stone, somewhat larger and of the same coloration.

"Come here, Kihara," said the storyteller to the person sitting closest to him. "Tell me, isn't there the same kind of rare flying-ant incision in both?"

Kihara clambered onto the large rug spread on the ground and held both stones against the setting sun. "I have seen many amber stones in my life with all kinds of incisions, but nothing like these. They can only be from the same location."

"I received the first stone from Matúzs when he was still living among us because I took on the instruction of his pupils while he was traveling. I thought the merchant must also have gotten this amber from Matúzs. I tried to recollect everything the merchant said about his journey from the sunset city. Soon I was able to see nearly all his steps so clearly that I was certain if I followed them I would find Matúzs and the two children at the site of the amber stones, should the children still be alive and with him."

"And you told no one? I would have been pleased

to accompany you, Kió," someone called, joined by many others.

"Why didn't you take me along too?"

"I would certainly have let Matúzs have it!"

"Don't forget, by that time anyone taking on finding the innocents after so many years was considered to be somewhat crazy," answered Kió to those butting in.

Mahanna spoke next: "You told stories through half the night for weeks on end upon coming home from less interesting adventures. Why didn't you say a word about this one?"

"Because I came upon them," admitted Kió, but his subsequent words were smothered by the crowd's outcry.

Mahanna ordered quiet with the help of a horn, then, outraged, she reprimanded Kió.

"Do you know what you're saying? Is this a fairy tale? If you found the innocents, it would have been your duty to account for your every step so we could bring them back."

"I kept quiet because I was afraid I couldn't prevent you from doing just that."

A man, shaking his fist, yelled: "How do you come to decide whether we should bring them back? Do you know who I am? Markara-gyó, father of the kidnapped boy! And I demand," he said, turning to the Grand Dames, "that we bring them back immediately! And that scoundrel Matúzs must get his just punishment at last!"

"But we already exiled him! We have no jurisdiction over him anymore," yelled Mahanna over the uproar of the others.

"I have a right to demand such! I have a right!" Markara raged on, ever more insistently. In the end his wife pulled him down.

"Continue, Kió!" said Mahanna, in a friendlier tone. "We must listen to the end in order to decide what to do."

"Thank you," the storyteller bowed his head. "Yes, we anticipated the innocents' return, but I no longer met innocent babes; rather, grownup youths who believed themselves to be the first and only human pair, and, moreover, of Matúzs' creation...," another loud outcry roiled up, but Kió raised his voice, "... whose offspring would populate..."

Cain jumped up excitedly because all of this sounded so familiar. Kió quickly got off the storyteller rock and, embracing the stunned youth vigorously, continued:

"Matúzs named the kidnapped children Adam and Eve, who, as perhaps you can guess from Cain's reaction, happen to be his parents."

It was fortunate that Cain stood next to Kió, because without his support he would have fallen.

"Then you are my grandchild!" said Markara, running toward Cain, "and this is your grandmother," motioning for his wife to come closer.

"Then I... then I...," stammered Cain.

"Yes, son, you are one of us!" exclaimed Mahanna ceremonially.

Later, many attested that they saw tears glisten in the Grand Dame's eyes before she completed her words of welcome, thereby fulfilling her official duties.

"If Kio-gyó is telling the truth, you are a Nódian... and I know him well. Even if he does exaggerate in his stories at times, in essence they are always true. Do you see?" she said, turning to the multitude of Nódians. "If not the kidnapped children, at least their child found his way home to us. But let us leave the celebration for later. Kió, if you don't finish your story, how are we to sleep tonight?"

"Yes, the two similar ambers opened my eyes. I saw once again what Matúzs, sitting on this very rock, told us about the island with rich flowering meadows, fruit-laden trees, peaceful animals guarded by seemingly impassable rivers hiding reptilian monsters. I remembered storyteller Matúzs' words: 'No man had set foot there before me, that is certain, because I came upon amber stones so large that any merchant worthy of his trade would have given anything for them.'

"I started out immediately," continued Kió. "Traveling from quarter moon to quarter moon I reached the Euphrates. Frightening reptiles watched my every step from its immense currents. Fortunately, I remembered that Matúzs was only able to find a passable crossing toward the end of the arid season. I waited until the river abated, just as Matúzs had done."

Kió fell silent. Only after the people of Nód made him aware that his silence was putting their patience to the test did he speak again.

"In the meantime, the kidnapped children appeared before my inner eye in hundreds of images. Sometimes they welcomed me with open arms, other times they attacked me or ran off. In my dreams they skipped along so effortlessly, and I had to follow them so quickly that I awoke startled, gasping for air…"

In the deep silence one could hear the labored breathing of the listeners, engrossed in his story.

"In the end nothing turned out the way I imagined," he continued. "First of all, in my mind's eye they always appeared together, and not as well brought up as the youths of Nód. I believe that Matúzs wanted to prove by them that if their mother did not spoil them, if the children grew up in nature, they would be fierce warriors in a man's world of male domination. I imagined the girl grown up in the wild to be a disheveled savage.

"It did not even cross my mind that the woman I finally saw on the island was one of the innocents I still imagined as a child. I believed that the appearance of female perfection in her nakedness, the intelligence and curiosity shining in her eyes, was the work of magic. I thought the hunger of my long journey conjured the apparition before me. Her shining black hair, her tanned radiant skin, attracted me irresistibly."

Couples in love and those already married hung on Kió's every word and drew closer.

"I was only able to feast my eyes upon this wondrous being for a few moments," said the storyteller, gazing into the distance. "Giving in to her attraction I took a step toward her; frightened, she ran off, disappearing into the forest. I vaulted into the branches of a bitter-apple tree to see where she had gone. Perhaps it was my desire or the loud beating of my heart that lured her back. She approached noiselessly, crouched the way a hyena scouts its prey. When she saw me, she cautiously stepped into the flattened clearing around the tree I had climbed. I did not dare say anything for fear of scaring her away again, nor did it occur to me that this girl, grown up in the wild, could understand my words.

"I leaned forward to see her better, hardly moving at all, but she disappeared again. I jumped down and chased after her because I didn't believe she would return again once she knew that her eyes hadn't deceived her, that I truly did exist. She looked back at me every now and then, and her smile was irresistible. To my surprise, she returned to the tree under which I had discovered her, resting in the shade. She was trembling but I could read curiosity in her face, perhaps attraction in her eyes—and also fear, as if she was ready to escape.

"I'm not making excuses, but as she had slowed her steps for me to catch up with her, then waited for me under the tree, and when I let my robe tumble down and the sight of my manliness did not frighten her away, what could I think but that she would take me as her mate?

"We stepped toward each other simultaneously." Kió's voice trembled. "Our bodies took control of us." He allowed a few moments for the imagination of the hushed gathering to take hold. Then Kió turned to the Grand Dames.

"Perhaps I am pronouncing a sentence upon myself, but I cannot keep silent about this. Even if I remembered that the object of my long journey was to find the innocents, the will of this girl-woman overpowered it. Will? Desire? I don't know. I am trying to recollect every moment so that I can reveal everything to you before you pass judgment. I transgressed when I set out to find the innocents without your knowledge. I transgressed when I gave in to Eve's enticing naturalness. But in my own defense, I was living without a woman at the time. When I gave in to the desire, I had reason to believe that I could bring Eve back to Nód as my woman.

"Her scream, her blood dripping on me, proved that she had not yet been with a man. Also, I could not have known that in fact this was one of the kidnapped. And if that was indeed so, what of the other child? Was he also alive? Was he there with her? Did the kidnapped ones live together as siblings?

"I know I committed a grave error when I didn't speak to her. I didn't think all of this through, but recalling what happened, I know that a single word could have ruined the unimaginable magic of the moment."

"Kio-gyó, wait!" Mahanna raised her hand. "This is no longer storytelling! You would have the people stand by your side so as to escape their judgment. Even if you had reason to believe that the girl had not yet given herself to another man, shouldn't you have thought about it beforehand? Weren't you more experienced than the young innocent growing up without women and girl companions? What could she have possibly known about the unbridled nature of desire?"

"You're right, M'lady! It wouldn't happen with me here, where our desires are restrained by traditions. There, in the Garden, it was as though time didn't exist. That encounter didn't seem real, or repeatable. It was only Cain's arrival that motivated me to disclose all of this. There are many strands of this story that I haven't been able to unravel myself yet."

"Don't even try, Kio-gyó! Don't even try!" said the eldest Grand Dame, sitting next to Mahanna. "Share the fabric of your experience as a whole, the way it lives inside you."

"So I shall, M'lady. I will continue. We lay drowsily under the shade of the bitter-apple tree when a man's voice startled us awake.

"'Eve, where are you?!' Although I didn't know her name yet I had no doubt that the voice was calling the girl lying next to me. Eve looked at me questioningly.

"'Eve?' I whispered. She was surprised that I addressed her, but then she heard her name again, this time much closer and more insistent.

"'Eve! Eve?'

"'I'm coming, Adam!' she said, rising and going toward the male voice as if she were only doing so to protect me from him.

"'Where were you?' asked Adam.

"'And you?' answered Eve with a question, perhaps to gain time as Adam got closer to me. Now I could see him through the shrubbery. He wasn't taller than Eve and could have been the kidnapped boy who, as we know, was one year younger than the little girl.

"'Our Lord woke me from my afternoon slumbers that I should destroy the evil one who has intruded into His Garden,' the voice came, alternating between a boy's and a man's. 'A foreign smell led me to you, Eve. Have you seen anyone?'

"'The evil one? Why did your Lord speak of an evil one?'

"'I will destroy him before he spoils the tranquility of our Garden,' said Adam.

"'Put down your club! The newcomer is without a weapon,' said Eve in a determined voice, but she was nonetheless more pleading than commanding.

"'So, you saw him!'

"'I didn't encounter any kind of evil one,' Eve said, feigning indifference.

"I watched in amazement, wondering how long this young woman could restrain her increasingly angry brother.

"'I can smell his scent on you!' yelled the boy. 'Out of my way, Eve!'

"'Until you put down that cursed club I'm not allowing you one step further! Even the animals who have become tame around us avoid you ever since you've taken to clutching that thing all the time!'

"'Don't change the subject! Don't tell me you oppose the will of our Creator, to whom we owe eternal gratitude and loyalty. Step aside!'

"Adam, who was on the short end of the argument, bellowed at Eve such that I was almost ready to jump between them, but she didn't require help. She continued posing questions to the club-wielding warrior.

"'Didn't you say that according to your Lord the evil one resembles you? How could this be, Adam, if He created you alone in His own image? And then only one of me, I don't know why or in whose likeness.'

"'Don't you remember, Eve? You never want to remember this. He created you for me because animals live in pairs.'

"In response Eve spun her yarn further. 'He always compares you to the males, and most males in the animal species do battle with one another. Don't you see that by constantly putting you to the test your Lord would raise you to be as belligerent as they are? Perhaps this destroying the evil one is merely His newest trial.'

"'He is here, I know it. Step aside; let me destroy him before he attacks us!' said Adam, brandishing his club. 'Believe me, he didn't appear in your dream. If so, I couldn't be smelling his scent.'

"'So what do you imagine him to be, based on his smell?'

"'According to our Lord, the evil one took on a form similar to mine.'

"'If similar to you, then perhaps his strength is similar to yours!'

"'Perhaps.'

"'And is it also possible that he is stronger than you are?'

"'Perhaps.'

"'Then perhaps it is he who destroys you!'

"This quick repartee was followed by a long silence. Then, as if another Adam were speaking, he said pleadingly: 'Why, Eve? Then you won't stand by my side? Until now we have always confronted snarling beasts face to face together!'

"'Didn't you say that with your rock-tipped club you can tackle the most vicious animal by yourself? Until you put down your weapon I will not let you near the marvelous being who found me.'

"'Marvelous being?! According to our Lord he is like me, he resembles me, and yet you've never said that I am marvelous. You've thrown my ineptitude in my face more and more frequently and impatiently.'

"'According to our Lord! According to our Lord! Stop with this eternal "our Lord," Adam! He is your Lord. Ever since I've grown up He speaks only to you. With His famous omniscience, which you never cease to praise, He never has an answer to my questions.'

"'And the stranger you're defending against me? Did he have any answers?'

"'I didn't put any questions to him. He didn't touch me with words. I didn't even presume that this winged being talks.'

"'He has wings? He isn't like me after all? Some kind of bird?'

"'I think he must have wings. Otherwise how could he come to your Lord's island protected by treacherous rivers?'

"It was good to hear how Eve kept him talking, but if their Lord appeared, he would certainly give his disciple power. I thought that, much as I didn't wish to do battle with Adam, I didn't want Eve to have to choose. I found another solution in my own defense. I grasped a branch above me and leaped up into the security of the bitter-apple tree's crown. Upon hearing the branch crack, Eve glanced toward me, at which Adam took advantage. Going around his sister he came at me with his raised club. I was no sluggard; by the time he reached me I had crawled further up. With weapon in hand he couldn't scramble after me.

"'Come, Adam, sit beside me on this strong branch,' I said to him. 'I don't wish to harm you. After all, I'm a guest of your Lord in these parts,' I said. He wasn't surprised that I addressed him. His Lord must have warned him not to listen to the evil one. He held his hands firmly over his ears, but I spoke loudly to Eve so that Adam would hear it:

"'Tell me, Eve, is the youth you call Adam your brother?' I asked, hoping she would say yes.

"'The Lord of the Garden, who created us, uses that word. "Eve, find your brother," He said more than once. Then, when we grew up, He became angry when I asked if

He knew where my brother was. It was about this time that He gave us the names Adam and Eve. He explained that He created us as a couple, man and woman, so that our progeny would create a great nation. But He didn't say what we had to do in order to accomplish this.'

"I talked with Eve at length until Adam's curiosity got the better of him and he uncovered his ears. He soon spoke: 'Don't listen to him, Eve! This evil talking being wants to mislead us.'

"'My name is Kio-gyó,' I said. 'If you are interested, I am pleased to tell you about the world I come from. Your Lord is a very knowledgeable person, but...'

"'Person!' cried Adam. 'Eve and I are humans, creations of our Lord.'

"Hearing his heated words, I concluded it was better that I not enlighten him regarding the one he considered to be their creator. Instead, I asked, dropping the tone of my voice: 'Who taught you to speak so beautifully?' It was visible on Adam's face that the praise made him feel good, which his words reflected only in part: 'Why did you come to us? And why do you mimic our kind words?'

"'These are my own words. I'm not imitating anyone. I have come from a distant land where very many....' I wanted to say 'where many people like you live,' but Adam had said 'Eve and I are humans' with such conviction that I thought his entire world would fall apart if I were to make him aware that a multitude of people lived on Earth besides them.

"'Adam, you could learn much from him,' Eve interjected. It could be felt that although they had many unresolved conflicts between them, a nurturing love also bound them. Can I separate them from one another, I wondered?

"His Lord will be here any moment, I thought. I can't separate him from his Lord, no matter what I say. I felt that Matúzs was listening somewhere in order to be convinced of his ward's loyalty, although it might not be loyalty but fear that motivated his servant to obedience. Fear that was absent from Eve. I looked at Eve wearing her nakedness with such natural beauty that I couldn't imagine her wearing the garb of our women.

"My ruminations ended abruptly, seeing alarm on Eve's face. Adam was kicking dry leaves and twigs around the base of the tree. I noticed there was a fire-starting flint tied to the handle of his club. He obviously planned to burn the tree down and me along with it. Only one way out. I remembered from my youth the power of the bitter apple's sweet-tasting fruit.

"'I see you would be capable of burning this tree,' I said, taking care not to allow fear to be heard in my voice. 'Perhaps you're not familiar with its fruit, which has a flavor that expands the mind and gives wings to the imagination. All knowledge will be yours from its nectar. A single bite into its sweet pulp and all your doubts will dissolve.'

"I threw him a ripe, red bitter apple, but he paid it no heed. Perhaps he already knew its magic dream-inducing effects that made the future seem like the present and transformed the present into a dream.

"'Are you familiar with the magic fruit of this tree?' I asked.

"'Our Creator, Lord of the Garden, forbade us to even touch it,' replied Adam. He looked up at me with hatred, but at least while he was talking he stopped setting the fire.

"'You can eat from any other tree but this one?' I continued, trying to prove the desirability of the illusion-inducing fruit.

"'We can eat the fruit of the trees in the garden,' said Eve. 'Our Creator allowed us to learn which give us indigestion. He only said of this tree, "Do not eat from the fruit of the tree in the center of the Garden; do not even pay it heed, lest you die."'

"Eve must have quoted their Lord of the Garden word for word, because Matúzs liked to express himself archaically when he wanted to impress something very important on his students. For this reason, I also answered in a Matúzsian, antiquated style: 'Assuredly, if you eat of the fruit of this tree you will not die, but your eyes will be opened and you will be like your Lord, with the knowledge of good and evil.'

"In the meantime, I pretended to be munching heartily on the juicy fruit, but did not take even a bite. I next hurled Eve an unripe one, whose poison is less powerful, and another at Adam's feet, much riper, but neither of them picked the fruit up. They were watching me as I pulled my mouth into an ever wider smile. Then Eve spotted an apple on a lower branch that was much more appealing to the eye, tore it off, and ate from it. She offered it to Adam, but he rejected it. I encouraged him:

"'Adam, are you going to let your sister get the better of you with her boldness and curiosity? She will attain knowledge of all that is known and unknown, while you, as lord over the animals of the wild, sink to their level.'

"At which Adam grabbed the bitter apple from Eve's hand, stuffed it whole into his mouth, and looked up at me. His angry countenance immediately softened, extending into a pleasant grin. He entered the world of awake dreaming, his boyish tumescence suggesting what he saw there. He looked down at himself, looked up to me, looked down at himself again, then cleverly wove a little wraparound cover for himself from the leaves of a nearby fig tree. Eve giggled and demanded, 'Make one like it for me too!'

"As to why, she didn't say, but her brother carried out her wish. Eve happily circled the tree with it, humming incomprehensible words, meanwhile glancing up at me. I was able to revel in her beauty the whole time.

"Adam got past the intoxication of the bitter apple and seemed to be drifting off to sleep. I was about to climb down from the tree when the white-bearded Lord of the Garden appeared at the edge of the clearing.

"'Adam, where are you?' he angrily called to the slumbering Adam. 'Why didn't you do as I commanded?'

"I clearly recognized Matúzs, although he seemed older than I remembered, having added twelve years to the face I once knew well. He looked up at the tree. He may have known I was there but he continued to address Adam, questioning him angrily as to why he had covered himself.

"Adam answered a bit foggily: 'Eve, who You made to stand beside me, gave me the fruit from this tree to eat.'

"Matúzs turned to Eve. 'What did you do?' he asked curtly.

"'Winged Kio-gyó enchanted me that I should partake,' said Eve, looking up at me and smiling apologetically.

"'Because you committed this deed may you be cursed among all the animals and all the beasts of the field. May you crawl on your belly and eat dust all the days of your life!' boomed Matúzs, looking up at me. As if that wasn't enough, he spat.

"'I am Kio-gyó, your dear pupil,' I answered, introducing myself in the hope he might soften his curse. In truth, I never did believe in curses, so it could have no hold on me, but I felt sorry for Eve because she looked at me as though my limbs, even at that moment, might be wasting away. But there was more to cause her worry. Their Lord addressed her: 'I will multiply the pain of your childbearing. You will give birth in pain, and pine after your husband, who in turn will have dominion over you!'

"Eve, thus cursed, raised her hand in objection, but Matúzs wouldn't let her speak. He turned his rage on Adam: 'Since you listened to Eve's words and ate the fruit of the tree from which I had warned you not to eat, may the earth be cursed because of you. May you live off it through hard labor every day of your life! You will earn your bread by the sweat of your brow until you return to the dust from whence you came.'

"Matúzs turned to leave. But Eve stepped in front of him and addressed him with the same determination she had shown with Adam earlier: 'This isn't right, my Lord. I don't understand—compared to what are You increasing the pain of my childbearing? When I turned to You with the anguish of my adolescent body You admitted You knew nothing about woman matters and gave neither comfort nor remedy for them. I accept pining after my husband, as Adam has pined after me. I just don't know what good it does if You don't teach my man what to do with his desire, and me with mine.'

"'Are you starting with this again? I have told you a hundred times...'

"'You said, You said, it's true,' the girl cut him off impatiently. 'But You never asked what I was feeling! Perhaps if You helped we could find a way to Your plan, the multiplying that You expect from us. How is it that You created us but didn't know, or just didn't want to tell us, how we can multiply? Nor do You understand that I am a feeling-hurting being. Adam was the same as a child, but You always reprimanded him when he burst into tears! And You even choked the love inside him because You valued that he please You based on Your command and not by listening to his heart. You cursed me, saying, "You will pine after your husband, who will rule over you." But I will do everything so that the second half of Your curse has no effect.'

"'It will be as I said. Forever.'

"'I had a sense You would pass Your curse on to our progeny,' said Eve, taking a deep breath. 'It will have no hold on me because I reject anyone's dominion over me. The trouble is that Adam heard it too, and the desire for power that You instilled in him, although I warned You of its repercussions, took root!'

"'Enough of this, Eve!' snapped Matúzs. 'The idea that you forewarned me how to raise a man who I created for the fulfillment of my plan—have you lost your reason? Is this the work of the evil one who stole his way into my

Garden and armed you with such brazen audacity? Curse you, you ungrateful woman!'

"'But You have already cursed me! Or is it that You now admit Your oft-repeated plan didn't work out the way You envisioned, and You now attribute having to give it up to our supposed insubordination? And that henceforth, because of Adam's trespass, the earth would only bring forth thorns and burdock for him, as if all sorts of inedible prickly and stinging weeds didn't already grow faster than anything else here!'

"The Lord of the Garden acted as if he didn't even hear Eve's words. This motivated Eve to vent further:

"'How Adam suffers because he has no hope of reaching the perfection You expect of him!'

"The one they called their Lord raised his fist and took a step toward her. I didn't know if he would have hit her, or if it was merely his incapacitating rage that led Matúzs to take that menacing step, but, despite his elder years, I had to prevent his harming Eve. I jumped out of the tree and screamed: 'Matúzs!' The force of my voice and surprise at hearing his name again after so many years halted the Lord of the Garden. Adam also opened his eyes. He jumped up, then recoiled as someone who sees a horrific vision. In his surprise he left his heavy club behind, which he had been clutching until then. I took it, not threateningly, just so Matúzs would see it, the better that he not even try to order

Adam against his sister. Eve smiled at me in acknowledgment and turned to their Lord once again.

"'Why do You think, my Lord,' Eve asked, now in a gentler voice, 'that we hide from You more frequently? I will tell You. It is hard to bear that we have to discover everything You didn't teach us about ourselves and each other in front of Your prying eyes, but that we need to know in order to reproduce and multiply according to Your plan. You only told Adam to learn from the animals, and that through desire some monster wanted to lure Adam under his power. Did You really say that to Adam, Lord? Because, ever since, he has become alarmed at his erection and sometimes even hides it from me. He yearns after me, without doubt, but he also fights against it, and so I can't experience with him what I did just now with this newcomer, whose unbridled desire embraced me so irresistibly that I felt I would perish if I didn't take him inside me.'

"'As I said already, may you be cursed, you common whore!' screamed their Lord. 'I raised you with great care and you gave yourself to the first stranger who chanced onto my island.'

"'The first? So, there are more strangers? And what are they? Perhaps humans who also speak our language? It's not the first time You made a slip of the tongue. But don't worry. I won't share my questions with Adam, who is napping again I see. It's important to him to believe he's the only man in the entire world. There's nothing he loves more than when I look at him as such. I will do so; it doesn't humiliate me since I truly do love him. I'm glad for what happened under this tree because I came to know the joy that leads from maidenhood to womanhood, which previously only caused me consternation and pain. I now look forward to motherhood with great expectation, despite what You said about intensifying the pain of my childbearing. I came to know that my body and soul are capable of endless rapture, that love augments pleasure and ameliorates pain. I would happily take on motherhood, but I am paralyzed in this Garden by the feeling of Your constant gaze upon us. Please, Lord, let us out of the imprisonment of Your Garden!'

"'Go then!' shouted the Lord of the Garden. 'But I will not remove my curse from you! Be exiled! Let's see what will become of you without me! Let the reptiles, my Garden's guards, eat you! Especially you, Eve, who brought to ruin the man I created to be beside you.'

"Eve stood immobilized, but then raised her voice: 'Destroy me if You must for my disobedience, but remove Your curse from Adam. He believes in You, so Your words have a hold on him. I'm not afraid of You because I have nothing to lose. My life here is no longer a life. I will fight You to the end for my man.'

"Eve gave emphasis to her words by stepping closer to the Lord of the Garden and threatening him with violence. Matúzs cried out in alarm: 'Adam, come here! Hold her back!'

"He screamed so vehemently that Adam awoke and jumped toward Eve as if to restrain her. Eve didn't even blink, and Adam stopped short. Matúzs stepped back, but I put an end to the escalating situation. I raised Adam's club to show him Adam no longer had it. Matúzs then turned and yelled at me: 'What are you looking for on my island, you embodiment of evil? May all your limbs wither, you snake!'"

Kió told the thunderous narrative so convincingly that the Nódians recoiled in fear, as if to avoid Matúzs' rage.

"'Would you defile the ones to whom I transmitted all my knowledge? May crows pluck out your eyes! Do you want Nódians not even to have a seminal seed when nations from the East, fortified under male domination, attack you?'

"Adam raised himself: 'Nations from the East?' He looked at Matúzs in surprise. 'Aren't we the ones You have chosen to build a great nation? Aren't we Your only human creations?' His Lord, mute and collapsed into himself, looked at him uncomprehendingly.

"At first I thought this was the appropriate time to expose Matúzs," Kió continued. "But I saw that Adam, even after hearing everything, wouldn't accept the truth. I had to speak with Matúzs. Turning to him, I broke the long, tense silence: 'Let me speak to you without your wards present,' I said. Matúzs, visibly relieved, sent them away.

"'I hope you admit that you can't take them with you,' Matúzs said after another long silence. 'The world I warned you about before my exile is coming, whether we like it or not.'

"'But Matúzs, in your long solitude with these two children, who you raised to be obedient servants in everything, you let go of your own identity. You have lowered yourself to the level of some kind of unworldly creator-god.'

"'If you turn them against me they will have no one.'

"Genuine concern rang out in Matúzs' voice. Ultimately, we agreed that he would fulfill Eve's request and let his wards go free if they could convince him they were truly ready for it. He would bestow his blessing on them and lead them out of Eden's Garden. In return, I pledged that I would tell no one that I found them."

"And have you now betrayed your oath?" asked Mahanna, incredulously.

"My secrecy lost its relevance with Cain's arrival. Sooner or later he would hear enough about the kidnapping for him to recognize his parents in the stories, even if I said nothing. He would have had to struggle to put it all together from random pieces, and I wanted to spare him that. Besides, Matúzs only kept our agreement on the surface. As we heard from Cain, although he made Adam lord of the Outerworld, he didn't set him free. Matúzs remained his omnipotent Lord. He let them *out*, but he didn't let them *go*. With the loss of Adam and Eve's sons, Abel and Cain, Matúzs saw his grand plan disintegrate, which will make him much more unpredictable."

"You can see that now," shouted Adam's father, Markara-gyó. "We can't leave them under Matúzs' influence. Let's go and get them as soon as possible. Cain would probably agree with this. Let's take guards armed with spears with us, in case Matúzs…"

"We will not take by force what we can't achieve with good words," Mahanna interrupted him. "As to when we go, it's up to Cain, since without him we would likely not find them."

"'As soon as possible?'" deliberated Cain. "My father would hardly be pleased to see me there without my Eve. I would rather stand before my mother with my own woman and child."

"Choose a woman for yourself, Cain. Afterward, let's all go to see my son!" said Markara, still trying to persuade.

"Don't hurry your grandson. After all, he hardly knows us. We have time to decide when to set out on the journey," Mahanna said, closing the argument.

"My story is nearing its end," Kio-gyó spoke again. "I thoughtlessly said to Matúzs: 'You can't keep these grownups by your side forever! When you die, the pain of loss and their solitude will be doubly intense because you closed them off from everything and everyone.'

"I became concerned, because Matúzs reached to his heart and acted as though he was at his end.

"'Did you come to scare me with my own death? You accuse me of abandoning my creations? I dedicated my entire life to them! I gave them all my knowledge; I will continue to live in them. Don't speak to me of passing. My knowledge surpasses death.'

"It wasn't his voice but his fear of death that was shocking; the creator's fear that his work remained unfinished, that his life's goal was unattainable."

"Wouldn't an aged and supposedly wise man as he take the end into account?" Kihara asked.

"Matúzs didn't purposely deceive his wards that he was the eternal deity above all else," explained Kió. "After he kidnapped the toddlers he had to mislead them step by step. If they asked 'where did we come from,' what else could he have said but that he created them from the dust of the earth, the way children knead play animals from clay? They learned everything from him; therefore, they considered him omniscient. He transported them to the distant past and future and they believed him to be everlasting. Mention of his mortality from such a lofty height brought him down. He was terrified of death. However, his old wisdom soon overcame this. We talked through half the night, like in the old days when, as his pupil, I sat at his feet. In the end, Matúzs harkened to a birdsong that I had never heard before, certainly not in the stillness of night. Matúzs replied in kind.

"Adam and Eve appeared with food. 'The time for Your evening repast is long overdue, my Lord,' said Adam, and all four of us sat in the moonlight and ate. Matúzs asked: 'Tell me, Adam, are you really prepared to be lord over the Outerworld, as you call it?'

"The question surprised Adam. Eve, to gain Adam some time, answered for him ever so sweetly, as if they hadn't argued earlier: 'Adam has never said anything about that because he's afraid You would consider him ungrateful if he abandoned You after all You did for us in our childhood.'

"I would have been pleased to listen to her soft melodious voice forever, but Adam spoke up, at first cautiously, haltingly, and then with increasing self-assurance.

"'I won't ever abandon You, my Lord. Never! If you let me out of Your Garden, I will remain true to every word of Your teaching and to You. Please don't consider me ungrateful if I say I would like to live and work in a world that I can call my own. You condemned me to hard work because I disobeyed Your command, eating forbidden fruit. A world opened up before me from its nectar, whose rapture didn't entice me away from You. Your curse was therefore unnecessary, but as You decreed it, my Lord, I accept that I should earn my bread by the sweat of my brow. Only allow my sweat to water the earth that I can call my own. I ask Your blessing on this. Even though You cursed the earth to produce burrs and thistles, I feel the strength in my arms, so that cultivating the earth will yield crops of which You will be proud and for which I will always be grateful to You. And since You have decreed that I shall return to dust, allow that the dust of my body enrich that soil which I can bequeath to my children. I desire no more than to be the master of my own world. After all, it was You who instilled in me this desire to rule. This is what Your teachings were all about. It will be difficult to bid farewell to Your Garden where Eve and I grew up, but we must do it in order to begin living our own life. And don't forget that You promised to make our offspring into a powerful nation. In order to multiply according to Your words and populate the earth, You must allow me and my woman to live freely, far from Your gaze.'

"With this, Adam got down on one knee and lifted his Lord's hand to his forehead. Matúzs turned to Adam's sister. 'And you, Eve?' he asked.

"'I will not flee with the newcomer who enchanted me. I ran away when I first saw him because I was frightened. Then curiosity called me back, and desire pulled my body toward him. You played a part in this because You taught us that there were no humans in existence besides us. I thought a deity had come down from the sky in order to embrace me. Adam and I talked about everything just now. Our gentle desire stemming from brotherly love was not enough to overcome our ignorance. But we have faith, my Lord, that free of Your watchful gaze we shall discover each other as man and woman in the Outerworld, and in this way our progeny will grow into a huge nation as You wish. For this reason, I too ask: please release me from Your guardianship.'

"'So be it!' said the Lord of the Garden, placing his right hand on Adam's head, his left on Eve's. 'At the light of dawn I will guide you through the Gihon Strait guarded by reptile monsters, and cherubs will meet you with everything you may need in order to begin life in the Outerworld. I have already begun making you warm clothes from fine skins, because nights there will be colder at times than here. You can count on my providence after this, too. If any trouble, illness, or danger befalls you, go to the rocky peak of that mountain behind which the sun sets. Call me from there with smoke from a fire that rises so high that I can see it from any corner of my garden, and I shall be there with you. But now we'd all better rest. A big day awaits us tomorrow.'

"This is how the Lord of the Garden spoke, and we did as he said. He led me to the hill in the Outerworld, and I waited there. At dawn, I saw Adam and Eve step into their new world. I knew Matúzs was standing there and I felt in my heart the pain in his. They started out through the shrubs, which almost swallowed them up, but in a clearing Eve, then Adam, turned toward the island once more. Shielding the light of the sun rising above the hill with their hands, they looked toward me. I stood on the highest rock and we waved to each other. I followed them with my eyes for a long time, imagining their new life. It never occurred to me that I would meet Eve's firstborn here. Cain, I welcome you! Live happily in the land of Nód!"

NINE

THE PEOPLE ENDORSED Kió's every word. They only argued about what he hadn't said: Could it be that Cain was his lovechild, conceived with Eve under the tree of bitter apples in Eden?

"In that profound bliss, Kió's seed must certainly have found a most readily ripe Eve," opined a woman who believed herself an expert on the subject. Others were perplexed as to why Mahanna-ma didn't ask Kió about it. When word of this reached the ears of the Grand Dame, she gave the following explanation: "Think about it. How much must they have brooded over this? Kio-gyó doesn't know when Cain was born, and I asked the boy in vain how many moon days or seasons before he came into the world had his parents resettled from the Garden into the Outerworld."

Cain wasn't preoccupied with the question of who his father was; he was soon able to rely on Kió to help him in everything, just as a father would. There was one thing always foremost on Cain's mind. No matter what they talked about, Cain always directed the conversation to how he could find his Eve, as he had earlier with his other friend, Kihara.

"You can easily recognize those who have not yet selected a partner-husband," Kió assured him. "They wear a green sign instead of a red one on their forehead. The same is true for boys of similar age. You will soon receive one yourself: when you see the one your heart chooses, you will know that she is your Eve."

Cain was happy when, at the request of his grandparents, it was not one of Nód's many virgins who applied the sign of Hunán to his forehead, but Cikara herself, the high priestess. Furthermore, Eve's son, or her firstborn as the elders said, became the focus of much interest, although he was bothered that many saw him as some sort of wondrous being. He didn't understand this, since he didn't consider himself different from people. He received a comforting explanation for this from Erhanna-ma, Eve's still youthful, richly experienced mother.

"You know, son, we people of Nód consider love to be a force that conquers all," she said, holding the hand of her recently discovered eighth grandchild as they set off on their evening walk. "We have met visitors from distant lands who hold hatred to be the greatest power. We, on the other hand, believe that a greater power is inherent in giving life, which love brings about, rather than in extinguishing it, which is reached through hatred."

She felt Cain's attention waning and turned the conversation toward his question about selecting a mate.

"We can't live in peace with one another without love. However, although we may feel this for a single man or woman, it isn't always reciprocated, and so can be the source of uplifting joy or equally unbearable pain. Yet sometimes this enchanting force captures two people under its power at the same time. Our daughters and sons all hope to experience this magic. They believe that if someone is conceived in such a blessed moment, a person capable of perfect love is born, often with magical powers."

"But what will happen to me if it's discovered that I wasn't conceived in such a magical moment as described in Kió's story? Almost everyone in Nód believes that I am Kió's lovechild, except for Adam's parents, who wish to know me as their grandchild. If it's discovered that I'm not Kió's son after all, can I still partake of magical love?"

"If you believe it will be, so shall it be. All magic originates in faith. And don't underestimate the power of curiosity, which elevates you higher if you fulfill the expectations inherent in it. Rejoice that your companions wish to get to know you; only be careful to always show your true face, lest those whose eternal friendship you seek to attain not recognize you later. And most importantly, take care not to cause disappointment to the one who accepts you as her partner in life."

Cain had lived the third full moon in the land of Nód when it seemed all the girls had disappeared from the city without a trace—with one exception. He knew that the others were there too, but he saw only one.

He caught sight of her on a caressingly warm evening, made more enchanting by the rays of the setting sun. Three girls were coming toward him. Somehow, Cain wasn't shocked that two of them disappeared from one moment to the next, or that his feet became rooted to the ground. He was embarrassed that he was unable to step out of their path; they had to go skipping around him, giggling and teasing each other about which of them had caused the youth to become paralyzed. But only one of them glanced back. She was his heart's chosen one; she turned, smiling at the enchanted Cain.

"It is truly magic," he remembered the words of his grandmother. "What can I do? Shall I run after her?" But his legs wouldn't obey his will.

He didn't hide his joy, least of all before Eve's parents, who took it upon themselves to escort him to the girl's family, with splendid gifts to demonstrate the seriousness of their intent. The girl introduced herself as "Mahal"; the name fluttered to Cain as in a sigh.

He next learned about another Nód custom. "With us, when a youth feels ready to choose a mate, he turns to the Council of Women. Beforehand, however, he must pass the initiation of becoming a man, which can take as much as half a year," explained Kio-gyó. Seeing Cain's dejection, he quickly added: "Since you are already of an appropriate age to make this choice, perhaps I can convince the Grand Dames that everything you have experienced is equivalent to the trials of initiation. Your long lonely journey through bleak and dreary landscapes from the Euphrates is in itself more than our youths would dare to take on."

The Grand Dames agreed with Kio-gyó. They accepted Cain for the selection of a mate, which was set for the next full moon. However, Mahanna had more to say: "Your grandparents, Eve's mother and father, came to me instead of your parents and said you are ready to select a mate."

"Pardon me, Mahanna-ma, but my heart has already chosen. Her name is Mahal, and simply saying her name fills me with joy."

"We understand, Cain," nodded Mahanna, smiling. "But mate selection is our people's joyous festivity. You need wait only a few weeks for this. If you truly love each other so much, surely you will endure our ancient trial." Then, befitting her high calling, she added with appropriate solemnity: "According to our customs, the parents of those wishing to conjoin tell one another all the troubles and ills, bad habits and expectations that can ruin their children's marriage unless they pay attention to them. Mahal's parents cannot meet with yours now, but you do not wish to wait until low tide in the Euphrates to allow for this. As a result, they asked Cikara to hear you out and, based on what you will say to reassure them, if in her opinion it is warranted, your marriage will be approved. Cikara is waiting for you in Hunán's house. Are you ready to talk with her?"

Cain didn't understand exactly what he needed to be prepared for, only that he was willing to accept any kind of tortured confession for Mahal. If he had any worries at all, Cikara's welcoming smile quickly dispelled them. She asked him to sit on one of the carved stumps of olive wood, polished to a gleaming sheen. Cain chose one obscured in the dark, but to no avail. Cikara took one of the torches from the entrance, placed it in a holder close to the boy's chosen spot, and sat down opposite. She looked at Cain for some time, smiling pleasantly, before she spoke.

"In place of your parents, your grandparents may speak with Mahal's parents, but they weren't witnesses to your coming-of-age, as was no one else in Nód. My task is difficult, since we know that many things can happen to us in childhood that we know don't live on in our memory, and sometimes resurrecting them can wreak havoc on our lives. This is why you must discover every deeply buried memory within you so that we may come to know you as we know every wound and scar of those who grew up among us. In order for Mahal to avoid hurting you, even unintentionally, she must not only love you but also know you."

"And I her, I think."

"So it is, Cain. But she can only see you through your eyes and only insofar as you can recall from the depths of your memory. This is what I want to help you with, my son. This is the art of the Nód Virgins. I am only able to hold your hand in your initial steps. You must traverse your life's path holding your Mahal's hand, holding on to each other during the difficult parts. If you open up to me now, Mahal will also see into your heart."

"I will tell you everything that has ever disturbed my days, my dreams. I want to do everything so that my Mahal will be happy with me."

Upon hearing this, the Nód Virgin cast her eyes to the cross marking the center of the colored stone floor joining the four landscapes of the world. Cain already knew that the Nód Virgins kept track of the passing days and seasons, the time for sowing, reaping, and festivals, according to how the light of the sun reached various adorned points of the cross through slits in the round building's walls and ceiling. They further divided the days based on this device.

With wisdom befitting the occasion, Cikara waited until a stream of light filled the heart of the cross before she quoted from the sacred teachings of Hunán. After each teaching, she lit incense in the flame of the blazing torch next to her so Cain could ponder what he had heard.

"The most frightening monster of the night can be tamed into a blossoming bush if you cast light upon it, and afterward, even in the darkest night, you may see it as a blossoming bush.

"It is never what we have already faced that stands in the way of our happiness, but what we dare not confront. Even in the darkest days of your life what you have already passed through cannot torture you.

"You, who have made such a long journey to reach us, and during it wrestled with your brother's memory, take a few more steps in order to shed light on even the smallest shadow hiding in your most distant past."

Cain spoke immediately, but did not get much beyond what he had already told the Nódians before he came to feel that the priestess was directing his thoughts. He was filled with a pleasant intoxicating sensation, something akin to a promising daydream. It was a good feeling to leave everything to the priestess, who led him to landscapes from his childhood he did not know still existed in his memory.

Cikara's words, coming from afar, awakened him to the fact that during his long pilgrimage many questions had arisen in him. Images appeared from his childhood. He saw the images in minute detail and was convinced that the Nód Virgin saw everything too, and so he only referred to the scenes in a few words.

"I grew up on my mother's bosom, slower, I think, than she had hoped. She and Adam had matured slowly as creations of their Lord. How could they fulfill their Lord's command to 'populate the earth' if their children matured so slowly? Eve would have had us mature like the fawn that, having lost its mother, my mother took to her bosom as my suckling-sibling until it gained strength. A year later it returned with its own fawn.

"My mother assessed me daily with an anxious look. Am I a stunted scraggly mongrel? Don't I wish to become more of a man—to be my mother's man? She encourages me to eat more, and takes me to her bosom again, holding me tight. Gasping! I must get a breath! I clench my teeth tightly on her nipple. To no avail; she no longer pushes me away. But don't castigate my mother! If you meet her later and listen to her, you will understand what she did and why. In her own motherless state, how could she have been a better mother? She could only listen to the dictates of her own body.

"I did what I could, depending on her for everything as I did. I felt that I had to break away from her, even if I missed the warmth of her body. I must breathe. I felt it. Somehow, I grew up.

"The other one there on my mother's breast is my younger brother, Abel. She does not pester him to grow. She wants to keep him as her child. She does not hurry him to become a man.

"How could her fetus grow to be so huge and rip open my mother's womb? Motherless Eve calls out for her mother, terrified. My father arrives in a hurry. Look at him well, because he does not dare come closer. I've not seen him up close either until now. My mother would not allow him close to me. 'Have you seen any animal who allows her mate to come close to her little ones?' replied Eve to my asking why. She does not even look at me between her screams. I go, skulking, to my father. 'You too ripped open like this from your mother's stomach,' he says. He does not comfort me with this. Will my mother survive? She survived, but she became Abel's mother. It was him she took to her bosom now—me only when I cried a lot and stamped my feet. Later, much later, it was not her milk I thirsted for. When I could no longer stand it, she allowed me to lie with her. What else could we have done? Don't look at me now, Cikara-ma! Release my will from the power of your will," pleaded Cain.

"My will only had power over your will for as long as you wanted it. You only allowed us to see what you needed to divulge. So tell us, are you apprehensive that because you combined the roles of son and husband with Eve you will be Mahal's son and not her man?"

"You have phrased that question in an odd way, but, in fact, I feel at times that my mother expected more from me as a child than I could give. Then I expected more from her as her son than she as my mother could give."

"Mahal's mother came to me because she is afraid that you are looking for a mother and not a woman. She did not say this, but it must have caused her worry that you always expressed it such that you wanted to find yourself an Eve. Eve is your birth mother, Cain, and she will always remain so. She allowed you to come to her as there was no other woman for you. Also, her only examples of motherhood were the animals. The ewe allows her son to be with her if he will be the ram for her flock. Your brother Abel wanted to follow this animal example and it was his undoing, because, as opposed to animals, who mature quickly, it takes us a lifetime to become a man or a woman."

"A lifetime?" asked Cain in surprise.

"Yes, my son, because achieving humanness includes all the great trials and experiences of our life. And, of course, the greatest test of our humanity is how we accept our mortality."

"We were always terrified of death. We did not even dare talk about it. The certainty of mortality was unbearably frightening to us because we had seen animals collapse to the ground, writhing, gasping, then stretching out motionless. If coyotes or vultures came upon them their bodies were devoured, or they decayed on their own; vermin hatched from them until only white bones were left. The animals grazed peacefully amid the bones, but we avoided them. We were terrified of living through all this, since we did not know when we would cease feeling. What happens to us in death's immobility? We did not know if memory lived in our disintegrating flesh or enduring bones. I have not been with you for long, but I hear you are not afraid of death."

"The fear of death lives in all of us. This is what keeps us alive. This is what protects us."

"According to my father, the courage that overcomes our fears is the result of faith in our Lord, which allows us to confront snarling beasts eye to eye until they retreat. 'If an animal's fine sense of smell detects fear in you it takes you for food, not as its master,' Adam would say."

"It is not that courage is victorious over fear, but that it allows you to do what you must. It is not only for facing wild beasts that you need courage, my son. It can take even greater courage to look yourself in the eye."

"And about our mortality?" asked Cain, but he waited in vain for an answer. Cikara's silence and encouraging glance forced him to understand that it was not so much his own mortality that distressed him, but rather that the hurling of a single stone was enough to snuff out his brother's life. Cikara allowed Cain to relate not only every detail of that fateful day but also what he felt, hoped, and feared.

While the youth who, in defense of his father, committed fratricide immersed himself in the event that forever changed his life, time stood still. No new beam of light approached the heart of the cross. Cain was grateful for this because he felt that, with every word Cikara listened to attentively, the priestess lifted a huge stone from his chest. It was only after he was thus relieved of his burden that he realized it was not that the beams of light vanished but rather that clouds had obscured the sun. As soon as he breathed a sigh of relief, Cikara spoke again.

"I see, Cain, that we have much more to talk about. Many things have come to life in you. Face all these and come back if the course of your thoughts falters. I have to tell you, son: I have listened to many a youth's story, but I have never heard of such a difficult fate as yours, who grew up in the belief that you were the firstborn human in the entire world and your mother was the only female human for the three of you. But I see that what you have lived through did not leave you wounded; rather, all this, as well as your long solitary pilgrimage, made you stronger and more compassionate. I taught Mahal about perfecting loving and the art of love. I know she will help you in everything if you will but allow yourself to be known. If you and Mahal need me at any time, come to me, before trouble takes root in your hearts."

Not long after Cain so promised the clouds dispersed and a beam of light engulfed his face. Cikara stood behind him and, placing her hands on his shoulders, raised her gaze to the source of light and spoke ceremonially:

"The eternally rising Sun has cast its light upon you. Blessed are you, Cain, as are all those who have saved a life. Think of your father, who can thank you for his life, and do not feel that Abel's death is heaped on your soul. Your brother could have avoided the stone if he hadn't turned toward Adam to slay him with a second blow of his club. You are doubly blessed, Cain, because the compassionate love that you felt even for your hardened brother, and feel still, is the greatest blessing humans may be awarded by the gods. At the same time, according to our faith, the love that grows to perfection within us is what can elevate us to be among the gods.

"Allow that in Mahal's embrace the love inside you, that for lack of another woman grew to carnal love toward your mother, may continue to flower. It prompted you to defend your father's life, which even your brother's conniving was unable to twist into hatred. Matúzs must have seen that compassion lives within you, which, in the course of your long pilgrimage, would become purified of desire's impermanence and flower among us to the level of divine perfection. Allow yourself love and don't forget: Hunán was born human but achieved the divine perfection of self-sacrificing love. You are blessed, Cain, and we ask that with your compassionate goodness you enrich our people!

"I will tell Mahal's parents that in the land of Nód they can find no better husband than you, because for women honesty is most important. You have proved yourself to be an honest man. Be at the mate selection! We all hope that you and Mahal will come to deserve each other."

TEN

Henceforth, Cain did everything required to prepare for the test of selecting a mate. By early evening of the next full moon his heart was pounding so that it ached. The women escorted him and four other youths recently initiated into manhood to the center of Big Field. At the perimeter, within a ring of assembled witnesses, five girls stood a stone's throw from the youths as they arrived. They shuffled in place impatiently while sheltering their eyes and scrutinizing their prospective mates. In accordance with Nód's customs, all five girls made as if they were deciding then and there which youth they wanted to "grab" from among the five.

"Of course the girl is only able to acquire the boy who does not run away from her with all his might, or rather, allows himself to be caught," one of his young friends, who was not yet touched by the magic of love, explained to Cain. "What always causes the people the most excitement is when several girls band together to catch a boy whose chosen mate is not on the field."

The newcomer did not fully understand this, not being entirely proficient in Nód's labyrinthine customs as yet. He received an explanation from Kió.

"If a girl only wants to give herself to someone in whose love she can trust absolutely, she can put her chosen one to the test. She may ask the women that she not go onto the field. If her chosen one finds another girl there so irresistibly desirable that he allows himself to be caught by her, our girls declare that it is better for this to be known at mate selection. If Mahal is not on the field, do not despair. You have won her if you succeed in running into the city for her before one of the girls catches you for herself. Only be careful, because those who want you for themselves, or at Mahal's request want to put you to the test, will be watching out for you on the side of the road."

Cain had no intention of allowing himself to be caught. He was mostly watching the two girls standing near the gates of the city who might block his path to Mahal. One of them wasn't even looking at him, but he realized that had he met her on his wanderer's journey he would have seen the fulfillment of his dreams in her and would not have run away from her even at peril of his life. The other girl, however, did everything to draw Cain's attention to her. His glance met with a suggestive smile whenever he looked her way.

As soon as the signal sounded, Cain set off at a tremendous pace slightly west of the gate. He immediately saw that he would not have an easy time of it. The girl standing in that direction, the one who barely looked at him, ran toward him, loudly encouraging the flirtatious one. Cain did not alter course, merely slowing down a bit to conserve his strength, and when they were about to collide he sped up and jumped to the side. He knew from the people's outburst of laughter that the two girls had run into each other.

He felt safe, and in order to quell his beating heart he again slowed down. However, he quickly regretted it because, glancing back at those standing close by shouting, he saw the coquette a few steps behind him. Her crimson face and heaving bosom would have been irresistibly enticing under different circumstances, but Cain regathered momentum and shook her off.

Once in the city many urged him to run faster, shouting from between the houses; children squealed, scaring him by pointing at his staunch pursuer. Their voices rang out most loudly, however, when, upon hearing their encouraging hoorays, Mahal ran out of her parents' house. As a girl who considers herself worthy, she had to show that her chosen one would strive for her to his last breath. Besides, it would not have been proper for them to fold into each other's arms in her parents' house. Since Kió had considered this eventuality to be so matter-of-fact that he

119

did not even mention it, Cain's heart nearly broke upon seeing his sweetheart take flight away from him.

When fatigue slowed his tempo, the people again urged him on, and Mahal slowed down as well. Although she did not glance back, by listening to the shouts she neither allowed Cain to close on her nor lag too far behind. Finally, not far from the city's distant end, she disappeared into a tent adorned with flowers. Cain flung himself after her and collapsed into her arms.

"Why ... ?" he asked, gasping for breath. Instead of answering, Mahal, following custom and the longing of her heart, gently peeled off his top that was sticking to him with perspiration, quenched his thirst with refreshing nectar, then washed his entire body with fragrant water. She motioned for him to lie down on the soft woven textiles and then, kneeling, spread oil first on his hands, then over his beleaguered feet. When her oiling reached further up Cain would have pulled her to him, but after a single kiss Mahal slipped from his grasp. She had oiled his hands especially for this reason. She did not allow him to speak, placing her finger forbiddingly on her lips. She then asked Cain to help her remove her clothes, of which she had put on more than was necessary, also true to custom, and, of course, she thanked him for his help with kisses. After the last piece, clinging to his lips, she pulled her love down onto the soft bed.

When in time she came to draw her mate inside her, she screamed. Loud. Louder than her body required. So loud that among the old women gathered around the adorned tent, even the hard of hearing could hear her, and help carry the news to the city that Mahal-ma and Cain-gyó had given themselves to each other forever.

Cain and Mahal spent three days in the honeymoon tent. Although they never saw anyone during those rapturous times, there was always fresh food and drink outside the tent's entrance. On the third day, Mahal's family and Cain's grandparents, along with a multitude of people bringing gifts, came for them, tossing flowers upon them, plying them with good advice and wishes for a rich life together. Then children ran before them, leading the way to a house that the relatives had built for the young couple.

After their nuptials Mahal could not get enough of her man's stories about the Outerworld, everything he had heard from his parents or their Lord about the Garden of Eden and what happened there. Later, she cajoled her sweetheart over and over with requests to enrich all he had said with colorful details.

Cain began to suspect that it was not merely curiosity that drove his woman. When he asked why she questioned him so closely, Mahal answered: "Why, dear heart, don't you think that practice makes perfect in storytelling too?"

"And what makes you hope for such perfection from me? You've enjoyed my stories so far."

"Of course I enjoyed them! But then I love hearing your voice even when you're talking with our neighbor about growing his crop."

"Thank you, my sweetheart. This evening you may hear a wonderful story about a carrot that grew into an oak tree."

"And I will do something with you, something even more wonderful. But I won't share it with anyone."

"Do you mean that you share my stories with others?"

"Perhaps you don't remember, Cain? You promised at Big Field, after the story of your pilgrimage aroused our curiosity, that if you became versed in the intricacies of Nódian storytelling you would tell us much more about your Outerworld."

"Is this what you are preparing me for? Kió too is constantly encouraging me, telling me that I will soon be Nód's favorite storyteller. He does not say the best. I imagine he reserves that position for himself."

"In our culture it means far more if we like someone

than if we hold him to be the best. But give yourself time, and you will be the best."

"How much time can I give myself?"

"In order to be the best an entire life stands before you. In order to fulfill your promise, according to many you are already late. According to me you are ready. Discuss with Mahanna when. True to our custom, the family of the one who holds story night at Big Field hosts everyone who comes there."

"Without the hope of good food and drink not even a dog would come to listen to me."

"Don't be ridiculous! We will have to start cooking and baking days beforehand. You are in luck. Instead of two parents there are four grandparents who consider you their son, not to mention Kió and Kihara, and my parents for whom you have become a son."

And so it happened that they gathered around the following full moon's welcoming bonfire to listen to Cain's stories. According to many, at times he even surpassed Kió. Of course he had an advantage since, in talking about a world unfamiliar to them, he could exaggerate, although he never said anything too outlandish.

They hung on his every word. He spoke about his

parents who knew themselves to be the first human pair, and their Lord who had them believe so, and his younger brother who wanted a kingdom of sheep. Of course Cain did not depict Abel as being as cruel as he actually was. For the peace-loving people of Nód he conjured up a shepherd king who, with his magical power, could entice the wildest ram into captivity.

This led to increasingly more people with growing frequency urging him to start out as soon as possible to see the kidnapped ones and the Outerworld.

After the fourth night of storytelling, by which time Cain had spent a good many moon days with them, Mahanna said: "Based on your words we have decided that we must give your parents, who were kidnapped from us, and their parents, your grandparents, the opportunity to find each other. We shall, therefore, send emissaries to the Outerworld soon, fulfilling Mahal's request as well, for whom it would have been proper to go before your parents prior to your conjoining. We hope that we can count on you and your friend Kió, for without the two of you we would never find our way through Matúzs' secret garden to your parents' Outerworld. As to who you will take with you, in addition to your woman and the parents of the kidnapped, we will carefully deliberate and then decide."

ELEVEN

Everyone hoped that the emissaries would start out for the Outerworld soon, and at least half the people of Nód found reason why they had to be among them. Cain and Kió were concerned that no matter who they selected they would be neglecting many. Also, they agreed that for Adam and Eve's sake, who no doubt still believed they were the first and only human couple, they could not appear with a multitude. And the arrival of an army of Nódians might induce Matúzs to carry out some desperate act.

To Mahal's great joy, however, she was pregnant and so they needed to postpone their journey. One postponement led to another. Five years had passed when Mahal addressed Cain: "You can see how happy it has made me after two boys to give birth to a girl child for you. But my joy would be even greater if we could finally visit your parents."

"It has only been a few days since you said, to my great delight, that you are again feeling the morning sickness that signifies a conceived life. You don't imagine that you will make this great journey while you are expecting?"

"Your magic always keeps me pregnant. Should I perhaps keep myself distant from you in order to fulfill my responsibility and heart's desire?"

"Your responsibility?"

"You know that according to our custom I should have given thanks to your parents for you years ago."

"That is a responsibility?"

"Custom binds, Cain. And better if you do not wait for the joy of gift-giving to become the nuisance of unfulfilled expectations. Even if you were not the perfect husband that you are I would still want to thank your parents for the intoxicating joy my lover offers me."

"What will happen if your time comes there, in the Outerworld?"

"My doula would gladly come with us."

Cain's woman found an answer to his every concern so that he finally relented.

"Of course I would like to see my parents. It will be a great comfort for them, the proof that my groin did not shrivel during the long journey," he told Kió. "What needs to be done?"

"There is much, and time is short. If we leave within a week we will reach the Euphrates when its waters are shallow enough to cross, and if we don't stay there longer than two or three weeks we can return before the heavy rains start up north and the flood covers everything."

"That stay is not a long time, but I imagine you have already planned everything."

"We have not planned anything behind your back, since there is nothing to alter in the travel plans we have talked about every year since your coming together. But let's call everyone who has anything to say in the decision to assemble here this afternoon so we can discuss the plan in your presence, my son."

So they did, and the doula stood beside Mahal.

"You have no cause to worry about Mahal," Doula-Ma smiled at Cain. "The women of the nomads living around us give birth to their children during perpetual wandering. Mahal is no ordinary woman. True, she suffered with her firstborn, but she brought her third into the world smiling. That little girl slipped out of her such that it was a joy to behold. There will be no problem with the one she is carrying now either, but I will accompany you nonetheless."

"The most difficult problem is that Cain and Kió have told us so many stories about the Garden and the Outerworld," sighed Mahanna, "that many have put forth incredibly ingenious arguments as to why they should be the ones we take along."

"No more than twelve of us can go. We already agreed on that last year," said Kió, turning to Mahana.

"Twelve. That may not be easy. Let's see, there are six of us here and the three…" counted Mahana, but Kió interrupted her.

"The children, the sight of whom we cannot deny the grandparents, need not be included in the twelve. After all, Hánokh is only completing his fourth year now."

"Selecting the dozen who may come will be difficult in any case," said Kihara, looking at Mahana, who reassured him.

"Perhaps it is not so difficult, because first are the relatives."

"Of course your grandparents are coming, Cain," said Kihara, holding up all of his ten fingers after having added four to the already counted six present. "Eve and Adam's parents can hardly wait to see those they have not seen for thirty years."

"Don't forget about my parents either," Mahal jumped up. "They should have met Cain's parents even before our coming together."

"It is better this way. We do not have to decide among those adventure seekers who want to come with us," sighed Kihara, relieved because Kió had asked him to organize the small caravan. "We are all in agreement, then. Is it not so, Mahanna?"

"I have to remind you of the decision of the Council of Elders, which they had reached when we first planned our journey, before Hánokh's birth. They found that we could only go if at least twelve armed guards accompanied us."

"I disagreed with this even at the time," said Kió, looking to Kihara for support. "Who ever heard of armed emissaries? Those in favor secretly hoped that we would bring back the kidnapped even by force. I hope no one thinks so any longer!"

"Most of us don't. But Adam's father, Markara, is always promoting this. After all, we are talking about his only son," commented Mahanna. "My fellow women are all against coercion. They simply wanted the guards for our security."

"Twelve escorts for this are either too little or too much. If the nomads who surround us see so many armed guards they may conclude that we have set out to do battle with them, and if they attack us in force the twelve will hardly be enough. If, on the other hand, there are only a few guards with us to protect our women and children from wild beasts, they will let us pass," said Kió, an authority on such matters, having traveled everywhere alone.

"I would object to our going with a large troop because of Matúzs. He would surmise that we wished to bring back the kidnapped by force, and we could hardly win his good will in that case," said Cain, adding: "Besides, we cannot free my father by force from the bonds of his faith that tie him to his Lord."

They discussed all this at length, including whether Matúzs might have foreseen Cain's arrival in Nód and might expect their visit.

"In five years, he could have organized the defense of his island," said Kió. "Beyond reptile monsters, fear of which he knows I have already conquered once. According to those who were once on Matúzs' side, he had connections with more distant peoples. From among them he could draw warriors. If he is truly in possession of valuable amber, he can recruit dozens of mercenaries to his island."

"That is possible," agreed Cain, "but I cannot imagine that the Lord of the Garden would tolerate foreign mercenaries on his island."

Mahanna finally put an end to the discussion, which had grown long. "Let six guards come with us who are also good drummers. Their drums will keep the beasts of the forest far from us. Their leader will bring a tall camel so that the sentry on duty can see from its howdah any danger lurking in the shrubbery-covered land. Another thing: we, the Grand Dames, have accepted the request of someone who has reason to come with us, but who wants to remain anonymous. Kihara, take this into account when you organize the caravan. We recommend that Kió lead us to Matúzs' island. In the Outerworld, we will naturally obey Cain in everything. Does anyone have any objection to all this?" Mahanna looked carefully at each person in turn. "Good! Then let us prepare for the journey!"

AND ADAM KNEW
HIS WIFE AGAIN;
AND SHE BORE
HIM A SON,
AND CALLED HIS
NAME SETH.

GENESIS 4:25

III

Cain's Return to the World *of* His Parents

TWELVE

Nearly the entire population of Nód turned out to Big Field for the packing of the caravan. Even in the midst of farewells they would glance toward the city gates from where they expected Mahanna-ma to arrive with the anonymous voyager. Their curiosity remained unsatisfied. Just as the horn blower signaled that the caravan was ready to depart, the Grand Dame stepped out from the city gate with someone next to her, whose face was covered by a veil.

The caravan proceeded at a good pace, to the extent that the heavily burdened donkeys' goodwill allowed. The drummers were needed only occasionally, as the cheerful travelers made enough noise to keep the curious wild beasts that appeared from time to time at a distance.

Only Cain was noticeably worried, because no matter how much he searched the surroundings he saw nothing that was recognizable. According to his calculations they should have reached the small clearing around the tamarisk tree where he was so pleased to encounter the little chattering monkey, but he searched for it in vain.

"Obviously we have gone astray from the course leading to the island," he said to Mahal. Kio, leading the caravan, turned around, slightly offended. "Everyone walks their own path in the wilderness," he said. "We are heading in the right direction."

After their evening meal by the fire Mahal recreated with movements and gestures the enchanting little monkey that had captivated Cain. Such playacting broke the monotony of the long journey. It also diverted attention from the mysterious woman, who had yet to reveal her face or utter a word that would have provided an opportunity for further conjecture as to her identity.

In three days they reached the shores of the Euphrates river. Kió recognized a few cliffs, directed the caravan in their direction, and they came to the desired crossing. Some would have welcomed a greater opportunity to observe the movements and habits of the dragon reptiles guarding the island. Since arriving at the shore they had seen only a few pairs of eyes peering from the water, watching them. From this it was impossible to read the intention of the monsters.

Kió, always in the lead, jumped along the rocks in the ford a few paces from the shore and immediately returned.

"If we follow one another closely we are sure to get across," he said encouragingly, but no one became more valiant as a result. That is, not until they saw the mystery person start off toward the ford and, without stopping on the bank of the river, cross to the other side. There, turning toward them, she took off her veil.

"Cikara-ma, the Nód Virgin!" cried out one of the drummers standing by the ford, and immediately started after her, but Kio-gyó ordered him back. "We are going together!" he said, brooking no opposition.

He lined everyone up on the shore, and they started off. On one of the rocks, which could only be reached with difficulty, Biko-ma slipped. One of the guards caught him before the current could sweep him away, but a small basket fell into the water, and a reptile pulled it down into the depths.

After the crossing, the exhausted travelers collapsed beneath some trees, but they hardly had a chance to rest. No sooner had they pitched tents and settled down for their evening meal than the miserable braying of the donkeys made them jump up, the guards grabbing their spears. Once the animals were quieted an ominous silence descended around them, as though even the leaves of the trees had frozen still. The customary sounds of the forest all fell silent—the ribbit of treefrogs, the swoosh of wings from birds returning late to their nests, the hoot of owls coming to life at dusk. It was as though the lizards, hunting for bugs beneath the rotten leaves to avoid the owls, had gone lame. Time stood still in the pregnant silence of waiting. So much so that they almost took the first sound that broke the muteness as relief. The sound, emanating at length, was like a reverberating yowl. It seemed to hide words, but they were only able to discern the word "caaarefuul" from the caterwaul. It was as though some animal-human wanted to alert them to grave danger. This was followed by the sound of haunting laughter, sometimes from afar, sometimes very close. Then came a menacing silence more unbearable than any sound, until the heartbreaking yowl returned.

Only Kio-gyó was bold enough to take a few steps in the direction of the sound, but he recoiled when he was met by a pair of flaming red eyes.

"Matúzs wants to frighten us off his island with his magic," he said, trying to calm his companions to no avail.

"Wouldn't Matúzs be able to make us miserable with his curse?" asked one of the drummers, addressing Kió and Cain directly. "According to your accounts, he caused the kidnapped ones misery too."

Cain would have replied that what he took to be the particular curse in question, "the earth shall produce burr stalks for you," didn't fully come to pass, but Kió gestured him to be silent.

"It's not worth arguing with those who wish to believe in what they believe no matter how unbelievable it is," he said, getting mixed up in his words. "It is better for us not to go on now. Someone who knows this island could put an end to us one by one in the thick undergrowth. We shall continue our journey in the light of sunrise."

The bloodcurdling caterwauling soon resumed, this time even closer and with words that were almost intelligible. The guards thought they discerned in them menacing horrors to befall them and their descendants. They convinced their oldest member to represent them to Kió and Cain.

"Swear to us," the guardsman, hitherto famous for his bravery, said, his voice quivering. "Swear to us that at the first ray of dawn we will leave this cursed island and return to Nód."

Kió and Cain looked for support in the dying light of the campfire. Only Kihara stood by them. Most of the others held on to one another, eyes closed at the sound of the increasingly portentous wailing. Mahal pointed to their children and with her eyes begged Cain to retreat, no matter how painful it was for her to forego meeting her man's parents.

They were about to give in when, without a word, the Nód Virgin started toward the blazing pair of eyes. Everyone waited with bated breath to see what would happen. The red light of the eyes died out; the terrifying screams stopped. They saw Cikara-ma's pale yellow travel robe recede into the distance and disappear among the bushes.

The rustling sounds of the forest resumed.

At dawn the following day, Cikara-ma, the Nód Virgin, was not among them. They worried about her fate.

"We cannot leave Cikara here with Matúzs!"

"We would trespass against the holy Hunán."

"But she went to him of her own free will."

"She sacrificed herself so that we could continue on our journey."

"Is this why she came with us?"

"Or perhaps she was driven by her desire?"

"She went toward the pair of eyes like a sleepwalker."

"We must find her!"

"Matúzs has no chance against our guardsmen during the day..." This was spoken by Markara, of course.

As the cacophony grew louder only Cain remained silent. He did not understand why the Nód Virgin had come with them, nor why she went to Matúzs.

"I must ask Mahal what is true about Matúzs being Cikara's eternal love," he thought.

He heard his name being called: "Where is Cain? He has to lead us from here on."

"Yes, Cain knows Matúzs more than Kió. He has to be the one to decide how we can free Cikara."

"True, I do know Matúzs better than Kió, but what we should do depends on Cikara's mission," said Cain. "Mahanna-ma is the one who knows about this. We must know why the priestess came with us and why she went to Matúzs. Only then can we decide whether we should try to rescue her from him."

"Undoubtedly she went toward the smoldering eyes for our security and peace," said Markara. "She took a stand on our behalf. Matúzs wanted to frighten us off either with tricks or magic. I can say this much: Cikara came with us because of what she heard from you, Kió and Cain, about her onetime master's blasphemous outbursts of rage. She understood that the one she welcomed into her heart forever in her youth required her help. Our priestess is a benevolent soul with a tremendous will. To dispel the devils that have possessed Matúzs will take time. It is significant that Matúzs has not chased her back to us before her healing powers could take hold."

"But can we leave Cikara with him?" asked Kihara. "If, despite her helpful intentions, Matúzs still banishes her from him, she can hardly return to Nód on her own."

"Your question is valid, Kihara, but the answer can only

come through patience. Therefore, let us continue our journey to the Outerworld of Cain's parents, where Cikara can find us whether she attains her objective or not. However, knowing her, we can be confident that if she can remain with him we will be able to see again the Matúzs she fell in love with long years ago. She has been hoping ever since that with the experience gained over time she may win him over, he who fled from the feelings that as a teaching master he did not dare accept."

"Perhaps Mahanna is remembering her own youth in her musing?" Cain whispered the question into his woman's ear.

They were soon on their way, with Cain in the lead, following one another in close proximity, their backs to the morning sun. It was difficult to grapple with the vines crisscrossing the trees. At times they had to unload the donkeys in order to pull or push them through. As they progressed into the center of the island their path became ever more darkly sinister, the overgrown foliage dense above them, blocking out the light. There were those of little faith who said they would perhaps never find their way out of Matúzs' untamed garden.

Cain shouted out: "Look! That can be none other than Adam and Eve!" and dove into the thick brush, unheeding of the barbs and thistles jabbing into his body.

"Come this way! This way!" he yelled.

"That's it!" he said enthusiastically as the others caught up with him. "It can't be anything other than the two cliffs my parents named after themselves and often mentioned in their stories. They always met here around sunset if they hadn't spent the afternoon together. They went from here up to the hill on the Gihon shore, where Adam dreamt of the Outerworld."

"Do you think we can still find the trail they trampled?" asked the doula, concerned no doubt about Mahal, who could not be dissuaded from tackling the vines that impeded their progress or carrying her portion of the bundles when they were taken down from the donkeys.

"Come this way, Cain!" called Kió, who had gone ahead to find Adam and Eve's trail. They found a path and eventually halted by the side of a sizable hill's steep cliff.

"My parents always recounted how they climbed on a hill overlooking the Outerworld," said Cain. "But Matúzs didn't bring me this way when he led me across the Gihon crossing."

Kió asked Cain: "This trail doesn't wind in any given direction, that's certain. What do you think, which direction should we take around this hill in order to reach the river?"

It was Mahanna who answered: "None. It's getting close to evening anyway. We will climb to the top of the hill, where Matúzs will likely not harass us. We can all use a tranquil night's sleep."

The donkeys were the only ones to greet Mahanna's decision with displeasure. Halfway up, before the cliffside's steepest section, they found a small grassy slope and would not take another step. Two guardsmen stayed with them and the heavier baggage; the rest soon reached the top of the hill. They immediately understood why Adam liked to watch the sun set from there. A beautiful world opened out before them. After the garden's dark primeval forest, the sunny open fields of the Outerworld, interspersed with flowering trees, some even laden with fruit, were very appealing indeed. Further beyond, deer with enormous antlers grazed peacefully. The cliffside of the mountain glistened like crystals in the light of the setting sun.

"We are standing above the crossing, without doubt," said Kió. "I recognize the place from which I saw Adam and Eve step into the Outerworld."

"I can hardly wait for us to be in the amazing world of your parents," said Mahal, snuggling up to her man. Yes, but the most difficult part is yet to come, thought Cain. He only shared his concern with Kió after their evening meal, when most of the others were resting. "I hope I will have the courage to approach Gihon's crossing, guarded by a cherub wielding a flaming sword. Last night, I relived what I felt at the time our Lord led me across with my eyes blindfolded; some misapprehension blocks my remembering."

"Don't you remember something? A sound? A smell, perhaps? Whether the ground beneath your feet was rocky or grassy? Anything that might help us find the trail that leads there."

Kió had already attempted several times to find a path down the hill but always returned dejected.

"You must remember something!" he said, sitting down next to Cain. "Only lizards can go vertically down the cliff's walls from here toward the river."

"I mostly remember my fear of the flaming sword," admitted Cain.

"Your Lord planted this fear in your parents' hearts when you were all still living under his captivity."

"It's possible, Kió. But perhaps it's easier to overcome the fear you inherit than the one born of your own experience. The thought of the cherub with the flaming sword standing at the foot of the hill will certainly vex my dreams tonight, if I can sleep at all."

"If we are this close to the gate of the Outerworld, it may be Matúzs' last opportunity to prevent our crossing," said Kió. "So let us stand the guards and be ready and alert!"

THIRTEEN

T HE TRAVELERS COULD not have known that Matúzs was no longer on the island. After Cikara, having at last consummated the great love of her life, fell into a deep blissful sleep, he crept away from her and hurried to the Outerworld to warn Adam of the impending danger.

No matter how much he did not wish to remember it, once at the Gihon crossing he saw with his inner eye the early dawn when he led his ward to the Outerworld, and he relived the pain of that fateful moment.

He was careful now that no self-recrimination should plague him for having raised the adult Adam to accept his every word without question instead of giving him a true education. Is a man in whom questions have died out truly alive? His mind, in constant argument with himself, insisted on asking if he had killed the true Adam by extinguishing inquisitiveness in him. He wondered if by forcing Adam to accept his every word as eternal truth he had crippled his thinking, thereby violating his vocation as a teacher.

"Yes, in fact I have violated it!" thought Matúzs. "Adam had become his own man when I allowed him to leave my garden; then, slowly, I made him my man. He was grateful when I set him on his path with my blessing, and I used his gratitude dishonorably by making him my obedient servant. Did I know that I would need his obedience?

"Yes, I knew that the Nódians would one day find us. I hoped that Cain would bring them here as friends, but they have come armed. I cannot allow them to take Adam, my half-completed creation, away from me."

These were the thoughts that occupied Matúzs as he continued toward his wards. He was displeased by what he saw when he found them.

"Why aren't you sleeping in the security of the caves? How often must I remind you that dangerous wild beasts live beyond my island," Matúzs called out loudly toward the couple and children sleeping under the stars.

Eve, who awoke at the slightest stirring of her children, answered him: "I imagine You are talking to Adam, since I don't recall when You addressed me last. But give me a few minutes," said Eve, standing up and stretching languorously. "We will move further away before You rouse the children with Your clamoring. You are calling out to Adam in vain. Even if You could get him to answer, he wouldn't remember a single word of Yours. He always falls into such unshakeable slumber after my embrace."

"Don't threaten again with what only you can give him, thereby placing your power above mine."

"Don't be angry, my Lord, but it's as if You were a continuation of my dream. Tell me why You have avoided me lately. Why do You only talk with Adam? What is that secret science You are teaching him? Is it that You want him to rule over me? Have You forgotten what became of Abel after he exercised the science of domination on his sheep? Or did You perhaps commission Abel in order to put Adam to the test with this as well?"

"Be quiet, lest he hear what you are saying."

"Let him hear! It's time he came to recognize..."

"I told you to be quiet! Everything that has happened since you allowed Cain to be with you is of your making. Tell Adam this, word for word: 'The evil one has come to my island again but now with many others bearing spears. They are coming to kidnap you. I was unable to stop them, even with the magic I had devised over many years. You should wait for them in hiding at the Gihon crossing. Then, without revealing yourself, lure them with every trick of your hunting skills into the center of the Ai-rom marshes, from where anyone who does not know the trails will never be able find their way out!' Tell Adam this is my command. If you do not pass on my exact message you will regret it. This, I swear."

Not knowing that Matúzs was far away, Kió sent Cain to retire with words of understanding: "You will have a big day tomorrow, son. Who knows what is waiting for us in the Outerworld? What happened during the night gives rise to the suspicion that Matúzs may try to turn your father against us, just as he did against me once."

"Do you think he knows that the two of us have returned?" asked Cain. They heard Mahal's voice: "Come here, my darling. Look how nicely my story has put the children to sleep, as if nothing had happened last night."

"Do you have a story like this for me too? I could use it," said Cain, kissing his wife on the forehead and crawling into their tent. "Perhaps it will keep the cherub waiting for me at a distance, at least until morning."

"Lie next to me, and I will have no need for words."

"Even so, I must find answers to many questions. When we set out on our journey I hadn't thought about the cherub, until last night. Even then, it was not so much Matúzs' conjuring but his determination that frightened me. And now I'm also worried about Cikara. I don't understand why, but I feel that the success of our journey may depend on her. Is it possible that Matúzs has ensnared her in his power?"

"It's more likely that Cikara has ensnared Matúzs, and that's why he didn't harass us further."

"Mostly, I'm concerned that after Abel's death and my exile my perhaps father came under the power of his Lord, your Matúzs; that he is obedient to him in everything and will turn against us."

"I trust Eve. Nód blood flows through her veins. Through the art of love, she has for certain tied her man to her. Even without other women as models, based on the example of animals, she chased him away from herself when you were born."

"When my father set me on my way he spoke from the heart about the joyous perfection of the relationship between *one* woman and *one* man."

"If only you had listened to your father! Perhaps then you would have noticed how much I would like you to partake in that perfection. But perhaps now we should really go to sleep. We are heading toward a big day, especially you, who must face the greatest fear of your childhood."

"Just for that reason I can hardly imagine that I can fall asleep. Let's talk instead, so I don't have to think about tomorrow."

"Is it really only with conversation that I can help you?"

"As your people always say: conversation is the strongest bond between two people."

"But we also believe that making love is a dialogue with the words of the body. My body has been wanting to talk to you for a long time, Cain. It seems to me Cikara fired up your imagination; let me show you what a good pupil of hers I was."

"So, am I right in thinking that Cikara also helps those who turn to her in this manner? If her body's knowledge extends to half as much as yours, I understand why those who know these skills of hers consider her irresistible. But tell me, who do the Nód Virgins help in this way?"

"They prepare the youth for the art of bringing joy, and they help couples who in the course of years have become indifferent toward each other. But in addition to this, Cikara is the most successful exorcist priestess. Of course, you are not indifferent; you simply tense up next to me like a pillar."

"Because you move around so much. Just tell me one thing: Why do they call them virgins? I heard that Cikara has given birth to a child."

"And many believe it was from Matúzs! But let this be for now. We have a saying that a girl is born a virgin and becomes a virgin again every time she gives birth to a child. I think it must be difficult for you to understand this, but you may understand by now why we attribute magical power to love. We can assume that love is a similar feeling for both a man and a woman. But a man cannot experience the feeling of giving birth. We hold that we not only give birth to a new life, but that we ourselves are born into a new life—that of Mother! This is not merely the emotional experience of motherhood. The gratification and joy of breastfeeding permeates our entire body and prepares it to relive the night of our virgin pairing when we welcomed our man inside us. But we had better go to sleep now. Your daughter will soon wake us, and you know very well that feeding her always arouses my appetite for you!"

FOURTEEN

THE FOLLOWING MORNING, they had no time for dialogue of either words or bodies. Most of the voyagers were already packing up when they emerged from their tent. Mahanna stepped toward them. "It's time you took over the leadership, Cain. Kió never came closer to the Gihon than this, but he holds that we can only get down from this hill the way we came up."

Cain agreed with this assessment, and once they reached the foot of the hill they quickly came upon a trail that had not been used for a long time but was not entirely crisscrossed with vines. They merely had to widen it here and there for their bundle-laden donkeys. The sun, at times shining through the canopy of trees, had not even approached its noon position when they rounded the hill and the Gihon spread before them. Not so much to the pleasure of the donkeys. Their joyous hee-haws attracted the gigantic reptiles, which began to convene.

They made good progress, slowing only when the shoreline between the river and the cliffs narrowed such that those responsible for keeping the reptiles away had to beat the waters with their spears and sticks.

"This cliff-face wasn't here," said Cain to Kió, who was following in his footsteps. "There is no magic that raises sides of cliffs from the depths of the earth. The wall couldn't have been this close to the river. We were walking side by side, holding the Lord of the Garden's hands because He covered our eyes so we wouldn't find our way back here."

"It's possible that the river has washed its bed wider since then."

"Possibly," said Cain, accepting the explanation.

Going around a cliff, a beautiful bay with smooth waters and wide sandy shores opened before them. The water was so clear that the fish, the size of a little finger, could be seen searching among the pebbles at its bottom. The cliff's row of reefs closed off the riverbed from the bay. The donkeys sucked up the water on their knees. Some of the people jumped in directly. Others only scooped water into their hands to drink and clean themselves up before they took out food.

Cain helped Mahal settle on the soft sand a decent distance from the water, into which he dunked a giddily screaming Hánokh over and over again. He then motioned to Kió to follow him. They had to find if the crossing could be reached from there.

"The soles of my feet remember this soft warm sand. I had never felt anything like it in the Outerworld. But let's see what's waiting for us."

Off they started, following the direction of the water's flow. Although the shore narrowed and became increasingly rocky it did not slow their pace, nor did the moss scarves that hung nearly to the ground from the trees. The squawking of a multitude of birds protecting their nests erupted as they approached. Then, from the thick woven fabric of the undergrowth came a hissing that prompted Kió to jump after his friend and grab him by the arm to pull him to safety.

"I thought you were purposely going to your death, you fool! No one has yet survived the sting of these slowworms."

"I don't know what you call a slowworm. My father calls them blackworms. I simply call them egg thieves."

"Their poison leads to a horribly painful death."

"It can't be so! They don't even harm birds. They scare them away with their loud hissing to get at their eggs without having to do battle with them."

Cain considered this sufficient to make it understood that there was no murderous intent in these creatures, but his friend did not seem convinced so he added: "Of course, they must eat too. My father taught me that they only steal one egg from a nest. Birds always lay two or three more eggs than they can raise."

"You may be right, my son, if this is the same type as the one you know from the Outerworld. But the poison of a reptile recognizable by this hissing causes such painful death that there is no person among us who would go near one."

"Stay here, Kió. I will catch one and prove to you their harmlessness. I have held more than one in my hand. It's not difficult to catch them because they have no fear, there being no animal that would attack them."

Cain disappeared into the forest and soon returned with a large lizard, hissing but not otherwise objecting to its captivity.

"Is this your slowworm?" asked Cain, displaying the black creature adorned with red spots around its eyes and on its nose, quite terrifying in appearance.

"Our elders say whoever sees one will never have an opportunity to talk about it."

"Nonsense," said Cain, and self-assuredly hurried back to the bay, but before anyone could see what he held in his hands, the lizard's hissing had caused everyone to scatter. Only Mahal stayed, holding her children close.

A few inched closer when he placed his captive in the sand, where it remained motionless. Cain knew that the lizards, accustomed to the darkness of the climbing vines in the trees' thick foliage, were blinded by the strong light of the high noon sun.

"Cain has paralyzed it with magic," said one of the guards.

The one accused of magic did not object; furthermore, he allowed his son Hánokh to take the lizard in his hands.

The braver among them crept closer yet. "Are there more where you found this?" asked Mahanna-ma, feigning indifference.

"There are enough. There are hundreds in the Outerworld, everywhere that birds nest." Cain portrayed the egg thieves' conduct in ever more colorful detail, concluding: "They'd be fools to eat the birds who lay their daily meal."

A good portion of the afternoon passed before they were again ready to start out. Then it was found that the donkeys had disappeared.

"It's not worth bothering to find them. They wouldn't come near such hissing," noted the chief guardsman. "Good thing I took off their load before we took our rest." Everyone was pleased with this until they got up to leave and each had at least three baskets or bundles to carry.

They passed numerous hissing lizards and none behaved hostilely. They began to relax and encourage each other.

Cain hurried ahead to see how far off his most difficult trial might be—the flaming sword. His grandfather, Adam's father, went with him.

"You can share your fears with me," he said, holding Cain by the arm. "To see my son I will stay with you through everything, and I can also help you overcome the fear in others."

"My parents believed, and may still believe, that their Lord positioned a cherub at the gate of his Garden to prevent them from returning."

"Do you believe that?"

"I don't even know at this point what I should believe. I saw that frightful sword burst into flames once when I was still a small child and ventured too close to it. Later I learned that the Lord of the Garden was your Matúzs, and I didn't have to think of him as my parents' omnipotent creator who we had to fear. Now, however, I see that many among you attribute magical powers to him and fear him."

"And you?"

"Others' fear transfers to us. The night before last I too believed that Matúzs wanted to force us to turn back through his magic…"

"The night before last," said Kió, joining them. "I confess he also frightened me. But now it is broad daylight."

"I would not have dared to come through the moss scarves hiding lizards in the dark of night," admitted Adam's father. "Yet magic does not reside in darkness but rather in the light of the moon…"

"In darkness we fear what we do not see, by the light of the moon, what we presume to see," said Kió.

"And the only monsters the light of the sun doesn't dispel are those living inside us," finished Cain, who was already familiar with this Nód saying. "But tell me," he said, addressing his grandfather, "can we persuade our companions to go near the crossing if the cherub is standing there with its flaming sword?"

"If horrific beings truly exist and stand in your way you must confront them; if you only believe they exist you must confront yourself. If you conquer your fear, son, the cherub loses its power for all of us."

Cain heard Mahal's urgent call and quickly returned to her.

"Why do you hurry ahead and leave us to ourselves in this scary place?" she asked reproachfully.

"But that was precisely why I went ahead with my grandfather and Kió. They helped me conquer the monsters inside me and so I may help you conquer those inside you."

"How many times have I told you, there are no monsters living inside me," said Mahal.

"Then why talk about a scary place? A place in and of itself has no power to frighten. But let's not argue, especially now. I'll send my grandfather and Kió back to stay with you. I must face the cherub alone."

161

"Go ahead, Cain, do what you must. I'll follow you with the others," Mahal replied, embracing her man. Cain felt tremendous strength in his heart.

"I must join the two worlds, the world of women and Nód and the new Outerworld, of which Matúzs dreamed," he thought.

Leaving the others behind, Cain once again quickened his steps. He needed to meet the unavoidable alone. His fear grew with each step. He thought of Mahal, the moment when he ran after her into their conjoining tent and fell into her arms.

"I could not bear my woman's disappointment of not seeing my parents," he said to himself, and with that his childhood fears dissolved. He took a few steps in his imagination toward the cherub that had lived so long in him and then realized... it was an enormous tree struck by lightning and blackened by fire that stood before him. Its sole bare branch, extending toward the river, shone in the sunlight like a sword bursting into flame.

"Or is it Matúzs' cherub pretending to be a burnt tree trunk?" The fear long ago rooted in his heart stealthily tried to return. Cain recognized it and fought against it. He took hold of himself and stepped so close that he could see wasps flying in and out of the tree's rotten hollow.

"A lightning-struck tree burned black is what Matúzs told us was a cherub," he shouted back to those praying for him. "Wasps live in its rotten hollow. It was their sparkling in the bright sunlight that I as a child saw from the far shore as flames. Come and be assured there is no magic here."

"And so, is a cherub not capable of pretending to be a tree trunk in order to entice us closer before it cuts us down?" yelled the oldest guardsman.

"You are not going to convince them with words. Come, let us convince them otherwise!" said Kió, who had caught up with Cain. Putting down his bundles he stood next to the tree trunk and urinated on it, encouraging Cain to follow his example. At this the Nódians started toward them. They could not imagine that the servant of any deity, even the most devoted cherub, would tolerate such humiliation. Passing by the tree they quickened their steps, and did not need to be told how to beat the water with their sticks. It would have been impossible to stop them until they reached the far shore, and it was a stones' throw from there that they spread their wet clothes on the grass to dry.

Cain set a big fire. "Let my father see the smoke from our pyre," he said, "so that he will come here for us to see him."

Adam had no need of the smoke from the pyre. He had kept an eye on the arrivals from the time they appeared on the far side of the river. He allowed them to rest around the fire before following his Lord's command, which Eve had passed on to him as they awoke at dawn: "Our Lord was here during the night, but His words did not awaken you from your deep slumbers. He left an important message for you. Some beings are coming from His island to us. You are to hide yourself at the Gihon crossing; then, without saying anything to them or their seeing you, lead them, with all the mastery of your hunting skills, here to me!"

"But who are these beings? What kind of animals could they be?" asked Adam, surprised. "Are they perhaps talking beings, the way that Kió was so many years ago? That evil one I was to have struck dead on command from our Lord before you."

"It's not our place to know our Lord's intention you always say, Adam. Therefore, do as I say. The message I gave you is His command. Go, search out how many of them there are. Hurry back and bring whatever you find in your traps so I can prepare a delicious meal for their reception. I'm going with the children to find something to go with the meat."

"How can you prepare for their reception if you don't know what or who they are? You can't feed the rabbit with meat or the fox with grain."

"The Lord would not send you to the gate of His island for a reception of such animals, Adam. It must be talking beings that you are to lead to me, so don't let their words surprise or confound you. And another thing: they are probably bringing a lot of bundles. If you can do so without being detected, bring me one, in which there may be robes similar to those of our Lord."

"All right, I'm going," said Adam leaning over his little son, but seeing that he was asleep, only adjusting his bearskin blanket before hurrying off. However, the little boy awoke soon after and, rubbing his eyes, looked after his father.

"Where is my father going in such a hurry? And why isn't he taking me along to hunt?" he asked in a complaining tone.

"A big day awaits us, son," said Eve excitedly. "We are having visitors, if you understand what that word means."

"Is it that bear cub coming back who we haven't seen for a long time? Perhaps it's coming back with its cubs, the way the fawn did that you raised."

"I'm hoping it's your brother returning, Seth, the one our Lord sent away. And perhaps that marvelous being also, who came to see us before your big brother Cain was born," added Eve. "I'm thinking of Kio-gyó, about whom I've told you many things."

"And my father too, but in a different way. So, am I to be afraid of him now, or..." Seth asked, more out of curiosity than concern.

"You don't have to fear anyone, Seth. But don't tell your father who we're expecting. He would be very disappointed if his son, who we haven't seen for more than five years, isn't among them. Let their identity be a surprise for him."

And so it came to pass that Eve heard the boisterous Nódians approaching before it was even sunset. So many human voices alarmed her, but with feigned calmness she welcomed Adam, luring them on as he waved from a distance to capture Eve's attention.

"They are sixteen, if I counted correctly, and three children. Two men wear robes similar to our Lord's," said Adam as he came closer. "I hope it isn't that one coming back among them who fled into the branches of the bitter-apple tree and was afterward cursed by our Lord."

"Don't forget, Adam, he convinced your Lord to allow us to leave the captivity of His Garden with His blessing." Eve felt her heart pounding in her throat: Cain is bringing his children to us, she thought.

"How could I possibly forget? You've mentioned it enough times. Do you happen to know why he came back? It's not..."

"Everything will soon come to light. How far away are they now?"

"Four, perhaps five stone throws away," answered Adam, "probably closer by now."

"I see you were successful in getting what I asked for," said Eve, reaching for the bundle in Adam's hand.

"When they went down to the brook to clean themselves I looked into many of their bundles. This one has a white robe like the one our Lord also wears. Could He be getting His from them?"

"I don't think so. Come, Adam, let's hide before they get here."

They had only enough time to take their two children into their spacious cave when their visitors appeared at the edge of the field, Cain whooping in the lead.

"My parents must have been here. Look how flat the grass is trampled! I told you Adam was luring us somewhere. They live here! I also smell food. I'm running to them!"

"Wait, Cain! It may be a trap!" said Kió, grabbing his friend's arm. "Don't forget, Adam's Lord did everything to prevent our arriving here. Let's settle here on the open field where we can't be surprised. Let's give him time to get used to our nearness."

Following Kió's suggestion, they set up camp. One of the guardsmen cried out, "Look! Is this some kind of apparition or reality?" He pointed to Eve in a Nódian robe in front of their cave, a little girl barely older than two years on her arm. A step behind her stood Adam with the first-born of his second life, Seth.

"Mother, is that you?" Cain called. "Who else could it be? It's just that I've never seen you in a robe like that. Behind you is my father! What joy to have come upon you! Is that my new little brother? And in your arms a little girl?"

Cain started toward them but stopped as Eve untied her robe and let it fall to the ground. She stood immobile in a dried-fig-leaf apron, proudly pulling herself straight as the embodiment of womanhood.

"This way, perhaps, you recognize Eve in me. Come to me, Cain, if you're not afraid of my embrace, with which I do not wish to evoke the past that I have long left behind."

At his mother's calling Cain rushed forward and they embraced. He next fell into his father's arms.

"And you, Kio-gyó, do you think I don't recognize you in your robe," said Eve, turning to Kió, who bowed before her as befitting a queen.

"It's true, 'tis I, even if time has left its mark."

"I knew that sooner or later you would return, but I did not count on it being so long. Are there perhaps even more people from where you came?"

"There are many, ten times more for each of your fingers. This is your son's woman, Mahal, with her children, your grandchildren, who made this long journey to see you," said Kió, pointing to them.

"Come to me, then," said Eve, spreading her arms.

"Where is the bundle in which I brought a gift of gratitude for my man's parents? I don't see it anywhere," said Mahal, looking around anxiously.

"A large bundle disappeared while we were down by the brook," said one of the guards. "As well as my spear, which I now see with the man who is standing behind Eve. Ask him about the bundle."

"The robe that I was wearing for your reception is from that bundle. I didn't want to appear before you in an uncustomary way. After all, Kio-gyó, you wore a similar robe until you found me and it tumbled off you. If you meant for it to be a gift, Mahal, thank you; although I must admit I felt as if my body had fallen captive in it. So, let everyone be as makes them feel free. Come to me then, Mahal!"

"This would be our daughter?" asked Eve's father of his wife, who signaled him to be quiet.

FIFTEEN

It was the first time after crossing the Euphrates that Kió had hopes of a peaceful night. Nevertheless, he asked the head guardsman, Hardhára-gyó, to wake him if anything unusual were to happen. "Don't disturb Cain. He has enough to talk about with his parents." While he was resting and still awake—or believed himself to be—Eve appeared before him as she did at the mouth of the cave with her babe in her arms. Then, floating above the ground, she left for somewhere in the future. Kió followed her with curiosity, but he could not take his gaze off her so there was nothing he could see of the future. At this point Eve's robe cascaded down and they were both standing under the tree. The dreamer was filled with warmth, but no matter how much he desired to relive what he recalled so joyfully, Eve disappeared and only Matúzs stood before him.

Hardhára poked his head into Kió's tent. "Adam sneaked around our camp and is heading in the direction we came from," he reported in a restrained voice. "What shall we do?"

"Wake up a few of your men, but don't place them on guard duty. Have them pretend they are dozing off in front of their tents. If Adam returns peacefully it is better if he doesn't think we set up a defense against him. I'm going to follow him carefully."

"Adam is a hunter; he sees through his back. You can hardly follow him in this moonlight without being detected. Stay, I'll let you know if anything happens."

Kió was certain that Matúzs had come over from the island and called Adam to him using the same whistle signal with which, nearly twenty years earlier, he had interrupted their conversation about releasing his young wards. Kió remembered with great clarity every moment of his time spent in the Garden of Eden. He attempted to use it now to understand what was happening. "At the time Eve stood beside me she too wanted Matúzs to allow them to leave the captivity of the Garden. Now, however, she would certainly turn against us if, in accordance with the will of Adam's father, we would try to take them back to Nód by force. Did Matúzs call Adam to himself to protect him? To take him to his island? In the island's primeval forest we would never find him. But would Adam be ready to leave his woman? Or would he sneak back in the dark of night and take his family under his care?"

Kió did not have to conjecture long because he soon heard Hardhára's muted voice again. "Adam returned and wants to speak with Markara-gyó. What shall I do?"

Kió was surprised and perturbed by this development. At one time, Markara enthusiastically turned against the women as an avowed and dedicated follower of Matúzs. Nevertheless, he forced himself to be calm: "We cannot prevent Markara from meeting with whoever he wishes," he told the guard. "But Adam cannot take him to Matúzs by force." Kió listened hard, but to no avail. Adam spoke to Markara so softly that their voices were lost in the void.

Kió hurried to the guard. "Did you hear what Adam said?" he asked.

"He gave Markara, his father by blood, Matúzs' message, and asked him to step aside so as not to disturb those sleeping. Of course I would have gone with them, but Adam signaled instead that I should stay and Markara nodded in agreement."

"Where are they now?" asked Kió excitedly. The guard motioned with a wide movement, somewhere in the field.

"Come with me! We cannot prevent Makara from going to Matúzs. Still, we must provide for his protection even if he leaves camp."

"Is it certain that Matúzs is waiting for them alone?" asked the guard anxiously, but Kió did not answer.

"We must get closer to them," he urged the guard, "otherwise we will lose sight of them in the thickness of the forest."

"Let's lie in the grass," the guard whispered. "Adam will surely glance back before he steps into the trees."

Kió obeyed. Hardhára soon signaled that they could proceed to the forest. Adam and his father had disappeared among the trees. Kió and Hardhára stopped and waited in silence. They heard Markara's angry, aggressive voice, and they carefully crept toward it, but froze when an enormous shadow came directly toward them. Adam was hurrying back toward the camp. Kió whispered to the guard: "Without Adam, Matúzs represents little danger to Markara, who is considerably younger than he. We can return to camp with no worries."

"The foster-father must have set a trap for the father who sired Adam!" said Hadhára, who felt it his duty to call attention to every possible danger on behalf of his charges.

When Markara learned that Adam wanted to talk with him he had hoped that his son recognized in him the one who sired him. Mahanna, Kió, and Cain, as it so happened, had convinced him not to introduce himself as his father until Adam was ready to accept that he was not the creation of his Lord.

"Adam may turn against you and will never accept you as his father if you are the one who deprives him of his faith," cautioned Mahanna, and they tried at length to convince him that it would be best if Adam were to learn from Matúzs directly how he and Eve came to be with him.

"Adam vowed eternal loyalty to Matúzs, who he believed to be his creator, in order to be released from the captivity of the island," Kió reminded Markara. Then he added for emphasis, "I heard this with my own ears, and Adam would consider it disloyal if he were to accept you as his father before his Lord released him from his oath."

"Kió is right," said Mahanna. "In order for you to win back your son, Matúzs must first let him go."

"My father was quite disturbed by the unexpected arrival of so many people," Cain said in support of the other two. "Give him a few days to get used to the idea that the deified Lord of the Garden did not create him as the first and only human."

So it was that Markara wanted to meet Matúzs; he wanted to convince him to confess to Adam and Eve that he had kidnapped them when they were babies from their actual parents in the land of Nód.

They were not yet visible but Kió already clearly heard Markara's raised voice fighting for his son with Matúzs.

"I'll chop you down with a blow, you miserable creature! My son is not your servant! Have you gone completely mad in your obsession, with which you infected many some time ago?"

"Infected?" snapped Matúzs derisively. "If I remember correctly, you were among the first to stand by my side. Furthermore, you promoted a stronger stance against the women. 'We men must assume authority,' you proclaimed, but you were only interested in your own power.

"Admit it, Markara, you too hoped to benefit if we conquered the women of Nód. But when it came time to take action, all of you deserted me and allowed the Council of Dames and Elders to exile me. You should be happy! I have given your son a way to become the Nódian founder of a new world order, a world ruled by men. If you were to stand beside us once more you too could partake of this power."

"If I stand beside you? Beside whom? Nothing has come of the great nation you anticipated from the seed of the children you kidnapped. My grandson, Cain, has been completely won over by our women. He has become a true peace-loving Nódian. Perhaps you could win over one or two guards to your cause, if you have something to offer them. That way, with Adam, if you can count on him, there would be four of us with you. What could you possibly accomplish with this many in your old age?"

"I have long ago given up raising Adam as a warrior. He can be Nód's king."

"King?" Markara was surprised. "There have never been kings ruling over us!"

"If you become free of the women, Nód will need a king with a strong arm in order to establish the rule of men, which, in turn, can withstand the expansion of nations already trained in battle. If I stand behind him, Adam can be such a king."

"Why do you think our people would choose Adam in particular to be their king?"

Matúzs took this question to mean that he had already won Markara over to his cause, and that he could reveal the details of his plans to him.

"I still have followers in Nód who we can get to stand with Adam. I also have men among the large Eastern nations who on my command can take news to Nód of an imminent attack."

"I still don't understand why our people would make my son king, since they don't even know him."

"That is why I allowed Cain to go to Nód. The stories he told about the Lord of the Outerworld have become legends. They attributed magical powers to Adam, did they not?" asked Matúzs with more hope than conviction.

"It is Eve that we in Nód consider to be an amazingly strong person. And the reason she became so strong is because she rebelled against you, while you succeeded in keeping my son as your completely obedient child. This is why I must get him back, to free him from your rule."

"Your guards can steal him from me. But he will still believe in me. He will consider whatever you say against me slander."

"Steal my son from you!" shouted Adam's father angrily. "You are the one who kidnapped them, you cursed…"

"Perhaps Eve's father could accuse me of this. You, however, well before my exile, enthusiastically stood before me saying you would dedicate your newborn son to our cause!"

"'Our cause,' you say? It was your cause! You wanted to win over power from the Grand Dames. You did not raise my son to ascend to power but to keep him under your control. Even if you could place him as king of Nód, who would defend him when those warrior nations of the east skewered everyone on the points of their swords?"

"I have a plan for this too, Markara. If the sunrise army breaks the opposition of the Nódians, the women, children, and of course our king, can escape here, where the

Euphrates and Gihon will defend them against the east, and Ai's swamps from the direction of sunset."

"It's a very good plan, Matúzs. But tell me—why couldn't our people flee the danger here before half of them got pitched on the blade of a sword?"

"You would flee before a fight? After all, it's not too late to prepare for battle."

"Even if we were to win the first battle, wouldn't the multitude of dead weaken our people? And the second, third, and fourth battles even more. Sooner or later we are certain to lose. What would have been the point of the first victory won at the cost of the tremendous number of victims? Now that I have found my son, I will not sacrifice him on the altar of imaginary glory. You know we are a peace-loving people. Come to your senses!"

"You will come to regret speaking to me this way..."

"Rather, tell us, how is Cikara? Do you wish to place her under your control too? If that is what you had hoped, you do not know her."

"Do you really believe that her skill has an effect on me? She was merely a girl-child when as my pupil she found a place in my heart. I had heard that she dedicated her life to Hunán after you exiled me. But then what is she doing here? I will send your priestess back to you in the morning. Kió may need her help. I know he is with you, but he will hardly live to return with you. Since his trickery disguised as wisdom got me to allow my wards to leave the protection of my garden, he swore he would never return or divulge the path to us. Whoever violates an oath does not deserve to live!"

"Cain could have led us here himself without Kió. I would have come for my son with my guardsmen long ago had our Grand Dame and Kió not held me back."

"If you wish to live and want your son to survive your interference in my plans, don't say a word to anyone about what transpired here!" The Lord of the Garden was so unaccustomed to masculine opposition that he was literally foaming at the mouth. "My magic surpasses your guardsmen. Do you see the deer that I tied to that tree?" Matúzs pointed to the little animal. "Don't take your eyes off it."

Matúzs stepped back and lifted a long reed to his mouth. Markara heard a soft puff from behind his back. The fawn cried out, stumbled, and soon collapsed.

"I'll whistle on this reed if I need you. Now, go! If you walk in that direction," he pointed to where Kió and the guardsman were hiding, "you will reach your campsite."

With that, Matúzs started out in the opposite direction with quickening steps. Kió pulled his guardsman behind a bush and kept him there until Markara passed beyond hearing. Only then did he turn to Hadhara.

"It is better if we don't say anything to anyone about this. Warn your men to stay visible on open ground. Beyond your guardsmen and myself, no one need be concerned about Matúzs' crazy fanaticism. I hope Cikara returns although every passing day she is absent increases the chance that she will exorcise the devils from her eternal love."

"May holy Hunán so deem it," sighed the guardsman. "I believe in the healing power of the Nód Virgin. She cast out the demons that had plagued my woman's father for many, many years."

SIXTEEN

Kió glanced toward the Gihon strait at first light, hoping he would not see Cikara there. He exchanged a few words with Markara when the sun was high. Without referring in any way to what happened during the night, Kió steered the conversation to Matúzs. Although Markara did not say aloud that he was terrified of Matúzs' magic, his fear was palpable in his tremulous voice. Kió also surmised from Adam's father's unexpressed words that he would do anything at all, even ally himself with the Lord of the Garden, to get his son back.

Kió set everyone, especially the guardsmen around the campsite, to carrying out insignificant tasks. It wasn't so much that he wished to protect them from Matúzs—he didn't actually believe that Matúzs would harm anyone—rather, he wanted to prevent Markara from secretly talking with any of the guardsmen who had been among Matúzs' followers.

Kió only loosened up when he didn't see the Nód Virgin approaching, even by the light of the setting sun.

"Cikara must have gotten Matúzs to accept her, don't you think?" he asked Mahanna when they were alone.

"Why wouldn't he accept her?" asked the Grand Dame. "She was his favorite pupil, later the only girl who touched his heart. Everything we hear about Matúzs shows he is taking his meager life without a woman all the more badly, although he would never admit it to himself."

"Do you think at his age..."

"The older a man gets, the more frightening loneliness becomes for him. It is possible that is what drives Matúzs, at times, to the edge of madness."

"Or, he still believes in the principle of male superiority, the inevitability of male domination." Kió chose his words carefully, lest Mahanna ask anything about Matúzs or Markara that he could only answer with a lie. "Eve was right. Adam has a hard time with so many people around. You can see he much prefers walking in the fields and forests with Hánokh and Seth," he said, to change the subject.

Seth found enormous joy in guiding the first friend in his life to every interesting nook of the Outerworld. Likewise, Hánokh taught Seth all kinds of Nód games, in which Adam was happy to participate, reliving a childhood that had been scant in such pleasures.

Adam had also discovered the pleasure of conversing with Mahanna. "You don't appear any different from us in anything; you are the way we are, like me and Eve," he said to her once. "Except that the Lord created us such that only I hear His voice and carry out all of His commands. Why do you consider it inappropriate that I expect my woman to fulfill my every command and wish?"

"You are carrying out your Lord's intent when Eve believes you are forcing your will on her. Is that not so?"

Eve heard all this and immediately stood beside her man.

"I don't know where your questions are leading, Mahanna. Adam has not been forcing his will on me for quite some time. I don't like saying this in front of him, but I learned long ago how to make him believe that I am obeying him even if I do the opposite of what he expects of me. Why would I argue with him? I love him, after all."

"The things you say, Eve! Especially in front of a Nódian!" flashed Adam.

Eve called Seth and Hánokh to come play tag before she turned to Mahanna again. "Adam does not want to remember that he admitted feeling played for a fool because at times I allowed Cain to be with me. He endured it without a word, never mentioning it while Cain was with us because he assumed it to be his Lord's intent that I be my son's woman. As for me, some inner voice prohibited me from allowing Abel to be with me too. Even though he was barely mature, desire made him nearly lose his mind, the force of which I knew as well, even before Kió."

Eve apologetically said: "I hope you don't mind that I turn to you with what until now I could not talk about with another woman." Mahanna took her hand, and Eve succumbed to the touch that exuded warmth and happiness. "Ever since you arrived I wanted to touch one of you. I now know how much I was missing, not only a woman's voice but also her touch!"

They sat this way for a long time. Questions that had been lodged inside Eve since girlhood came gushing forth. Mahanna answered patiently, kindly, denying none of the difficulties of a woman's fate but emphasizing its beauties, joys, magnificence. In the end, the Grand Dame of the Nódians managed to direct the talk to Matúzs—she had to decide if there was a chance that he would allow the kidnapped couple to return to Nód peacefully.

"Kió and Cain told you the truth about Adam's Lord, your Matúzs, having an unpredictable nature, quick to flare. He was not always this way. With fatherly concern He calmed Adam when he turned to Him, scared because, as his body became more hairy, he thought he would become a wild animal. As to my bleeding, however, our Lord turned away in disgust. He did say when it had already happened several times that it is part of becoming a woman. He did not know the kind of pain this or the swelling of my breasts came with. Tell me, Mahanna, does every girl...?"

Mahanna answered her questions, then Eve answered Mahanna's.

"It made our Lord happy when He could teach us about our childhood. But later Adam surpassed Him in tracking animals, setting traps, capturing wild beasts. Matúzs started to change then. He took it hard that He was no longer the source of all knowledge, that we came to understand many things on our own. Maybe it was then that He recognized He could lose Adam as a result of his growing up, the way He had already lost me. But tell me, Mahanna, with you, where so many children live together, more than I can imagine, does the father let go of his son with so much difficulty? It does not appear difficult for either parent among animals."

"With us, the girls never leave their mothers. This is why our society of women is so mutually supportive," Mahanna explained. "An adolescent boy, however, must leave his parents because 'the man-child leaves his father and mother and abides with his wife, and they become one body.' Our ancestors bequeathed this to us. It is what your firstborn, Cain, did and he now lives in infinite happiness with his woman, Mahal."

"Ever since our daughter was born the hope that Cain would send a youth from where he found his Eve has kept me alive. Even before you arrived I was hoping that my little girl would not have to be Seth's woman. I know how difficult it was to accept Adam, who I loved as my brother, as my husband. Perhaps I rebelled against our Lord's words, considered it a curse against which I must fight, because I could not endure that my brother had dominion over me."

"Why do you say it like that, Eve? Would you have accepted another man's domination? Kió cited the words he heard from your Lord's mouth and against which you rebelled: 'You will pine for your husband who rules over you.' These were Matúzs' words, were they not?" asked the Grand Dame, in order also to confirm the veracity of this witness' report.

"I accepted Kió's manliness before our Lord's curse sounded; my will at that time gave in. It was a magnificent feeling to be at one with his body, a feeling I could not experience with my brother on our first encounter; reservations and fears lingered."

"Your first encounter with each other? Was there perhaps a second one with Adam? You don't need to speak about it if it makes you uncomfortable."

"Mahanna, if you could know what it means to me to finally be able to speak to a woman about woman feelings! Yes, we found each other when his tongue loosened under his traumatic fever, which came soon after Abel wounded his arm with his maul. The wound festered and he became delirious. He allowed a view into his until then unreachable world, and it was then that my love for him turned into being in love with him. But perhaps it would be truer if I were to say that in the Adam who returned from near death it was not my brother that I embraced but a wonderful, strong yet gentle man with whom I could feel as much at one as I had with Kió."

"Kió and your son told so many stories about you that many of us women of Nód understood ourselves better as a result of imagining ourselves in your place. The Nód Virgins often say to their daughters and to the women who turn to them, 'imagine yourself in Eve's place.' They tell legends about your meeting Kió, as well as about Adam, and Matúzs' magic. There was hardly anyone in Nód, woman or youth, who did not wish to come take a look at you."

"More of you could have come if you did so without your guardsmen. That you came armed to His island is what made the Lord of the Garden lose His mind. What else could He have thought but that you wanted to take us away by force? This is why He wanted to turn you back with His magic, about which Hánokh tells Seth ever more incredible stories."

"Does Seth already know that your Lord is our Matúzs?"

"I taught him from birth that Adam's Lord is a nice grandfather. That's why Seth easily accepted that Hánokh calls him Matúzs. Luckily, he's a good sleeper so he didn't hear when his Lord turned Adam against you."

"What are you saying, Eve?"

"You were still on His island when, in the middle of the night, He came to us and told Adam to lead you into the middle of the Ai swamps." Thus Eve related almost word for word Matúzs' command of a few days earlier, and also how she passed it on to Adam as he awoke.

"So you dared to do this?" asked Mahanna, surprised.

"Why wouldn't I have? I learned long ago to discern from Adam's Lord's voice when it is merely His enflamed rage speaking."

"And can you still be certain of this feeling of yours?"

"Don't worry. At times His concern about us drives Him mad, but there is tremendous goodness inside Him, which He conceals increasingly from Himself because He considers it a sign of weakness. He never lost His patience until our adolescence. He changed most when He had us collect many egg-stones—amber, as Matúzs and you call them—and disappeared for many months.

"After He returned He growled at us for everything. He maintained that we had gone to ruin in His absence. We had become savages. I don't remember what I said in our defense because He didn't allow me to finish my words. He accused Adam of being submissive. I could not make him understand that it was not we who had changed but our Lord."

"Did you find out what made him change so, or at least where he had gone? Did he say anything about some sort of danger?"

"Danger? Threat! He bought arms, lances, clubs, two shields. He returned with a donkey laden to the point of collapse. He wished to teach Adam warrior skills. He wanted Adam to attack Him and He would defend Himself with the shield. Adam was incapable of raising a weapon against Him; it was as if his arm had become paralyzed. The Lord of the Garden screamed in vain for him to strike Him down. He would deflect the blows with His shield. He could only get Adam to defend, which he did so well that Matúzs' bludgeoning blows soon shattered both shields.

"Did Matúzs give up teaching him armed combat?"

"What else could He have done? And as this happened not long before your Kio-gyó arrived here and our Lord released us from His Garden's imprisonment, there was little time to indoctrinate Adam."

"According to Cain, Adam's Lord also came to the Outerworld frequently to see Adam. Didn't he try to continue teaching him there?"

"Not with weapons, but He talked to him many times about the mastery of leadership. Usually He did this when He believed I couldn't hear Him. Only now am I beginning to realize that He did not want to talk of this in front of me because by then I had asked Him many times if there were other humans living somewhere beyond the Euphrates. I was certain that there were women living where Kió came from; otherwise, how would he have known what he wanted to do with me? Adam and I tried in vain, and we didn't think he could penetrate me where only blood flowed out of me."

Eve looked at Mahanna with concern. "I hope I do not embarrass you with this the way I did Matúzs. If I remember well, He mumbled something about woman's fate, but He did not believe how much at times my belly ached. I begged Him, but He didn't make a potion for me from His carefully guarded roots."

"Don't blame Matúzs. The potions with which he helped heal ailments from bad edibles would hardly have diminished your woman's pains."

"He had medications for everything else. For Adam's wound, too. We watched over Adam together, cleaning his wound with potions, soothing his fever with cold spring water. Meanwhile, of course, we talked a lot, especially about what Adam mumbled in his fever regarding Cain. He saw him fighting monsters in faraway lands. At times, he shouted out to alert him to dangers, or implored his Lord to defend Cain. Matúzs reassured Adam that He was present with his son, safeguarding his every step."

"That's what he said?"

"Yes, and I understand what's behind your question. Perhaps I did not express myself well. I am certain that He did not simply want to convince Adam of His Omnipotence. Nevertheless, that is what He also did; His face almost always floated above my incapacitated man's face. There were times when I was afraid of Him..." Eve's voice trailed off.

"Did he ever speak of Hunán, our chief god, to the two of you?"

"In our childhood He told us stories of marvelous omniscient beings living on the tops of high mountains. He may have mentioned your Hunán among them, but the one thing I remember is our Lord pronounced his name as "Hu-naan." As we were growing up, He didn't like it if we brought these stories up for discussion. 'We must believe in ourselves,' He would say. We always thought that He included Himself in the 'ourselves.'"

"Our chief god's ancient name is 'Hunaan,' which means 'Spirit that stands above or exists over everything' in the language very few still remember. We believe that the Spirit of our ancestors lives with us. Among every large family's ancestors there is one or more whose Spirit is regarded as a deity. But all of us honor Hunán as god above all, who left us with many wise teachings."

"Do you mean that Hu-naan or Hunán was once a living person among you and only later became a god?"

"All peoples have their gods. There are those who believe that their gods sometimes descend to walk among them from the lofty heavens or from mountain peaks. Then there are those, including us, who believe there are people living among us who approximate godlike perfection and their Spirit, released from their decaying bodies, can ascend to be with the gods. We believe the Spirit of all our ancestors lives among us, but there are Spirits who also have free entry into the world of the gods."

Eve considered: "At times we gleaned from our Lord's stories that He lived some time ago among marvelous beings. In our childhood, we imagined that He descended from a mountain peak that reached to the heavens in order to create us. Later, when He became increasingly impatient with us, I thought to myself that He regretted not staying up there. I was sorry to have disappointed Him when I changed so much in my adolescence, but my trying not to change was futile."

At Mahanna's request, Eve returned to her story of the benevolent, healing Matúzs.

"We were already living in a spacious cave at the time. Adam made it habitable. He filled in the stone slabs on the cave's floor with soil that he pounded hard. We loved its depth, comfortably warm on the coldest nights and cool during the hottest days. The rising sun lit it each morning.

I mention this because after a night of sleeplessness, coming to wakefulness after finally dozing off, I saw a divine being descending with our Lord's face, resplendent in its caretaking goodness, a golden wreath from the sun in His hair."

"Do you think Adam may have seen his Lord in this way, in such glory? But wait, Eve! Cain too would certainly like to know this." Mahanna stood to leave, but Eve did not let go of her hand. Rather, she begged: "Stay! There is something I would not be able to talk about in front of Adam or Cain. But let me say that our Lord truly brought my man back from death; he was already smelling.

"When Adam was reborn, he required our caretaking for a long time. I only left him with his Lord when I went for food. I had learned the use of traps to some extent. I procured what the three of us needed while Adam couldn't even get up. Then he went out one dawn and brought back a hunter's goodly haul. We celebrated his recovery and our Lord returned to His island.

"This is when Adam and I found each other, no longer fumbling like siblings. I soon felt the beginning of a life inside me. It dawned on me that my firstborn might not be Adam's but Kió's progeny, but something whispered it was better that Adam not know. It hurt that I was keeping a secret from the one with whom I often became one body.

But I am pleased to talk with you about this. It is as if you have already taken upon yourself half the burden of my secret."

"Perhaps I can also alleviate half the burden you are still carrying if I tell you what Cain has known for a long time. We Nódians consider a child's father to be the one who actually raises the child. A man plants his seed inside us to his joy and pleasure, perhaps not even thinking of procreation, and nature does not wish for him to feel when his seed impregnates us. Conception is always our secret, Eve, our joy and responsibility, including how and with whom we share this joy."

"Does Cain know or suspect that Kió might be his father? If not, should he know?"

"Kió told the story of your meeting. Also, that he hoped he could bring you to Nód. Later he convinced Matúzs to let you come here, to the Outerworld. Kió told us all of this in order to convince us that Cain is a son of Nód. Whether it was Adam or Kió who sired him changes nothing."

"My son is a son of Nód, you say. This evokes the feeling that came over me when I first saw your guardsmen, who perhaps I should have feared. Instead, I felt them to be my sons. I put on the garment I acquired from you because I did not wish to appear before you as Eve. I suspected that it was not only our Lord and Kió who wore the white caftan.

I wanted to appear similar to you all, but I could not remain as someone I am not. I could not abide the imprisonment of the robe I put on and it tumbled off me. I accepted what according to our Lord's teachings I knew myself to be: Eve, the mother of every person."

"That is also how we saw you there, your little girl in your arms, the mother of future generations. We all felt amazing power emanating from you."

"Our Lord also always said that I should hold Adam's hand burning with fever in my own and allow my strength to flow into his debilitated body. Although, without our Lord's healing…"

"I'm telling you, Eve, we all must hear about Matúzs' healing goodness. Especially those who still wish to condemn him for kidnapping."

"Adam always said that the ways of his Lord are unfathomable. Tell me, Mahanna, how much longer must we keep secret from Adam about who his Lord actually is?"

"We agreed to wait until Matúzs comes here and can talk about it."

"That's true, but, at the time, we thought your priestess would bring the newly reborn Matúzs here in a day or two."

"Believe me, Eve, the later they come the better. Cikara's exorcism science often works slowly, especially when the possessed is not ready to let go of his devils. In the meantime, let us prepare. This storytelling evening will be yours."

SEVENTEEN

"Mahanna asked me to tell you what happened after, on the advice of our Lord, my firstborn, Cain, had to leave us." Thus Eve began her story. She turned to Cain: "After you left us, son, with a great ache in my heart I went with Adam to look at Abel's body. We took his body to the safety of a nearby cave, and I closed off its mouth with rocks. Adam's wounded arm was so swollen by this time that he was unable to use it. Then he was overcome by such fever that I could barely get him up to our cave. I was also frightened by his saying something I had never heard before, as if he did not really intend his words for me. Perhaps he didn't even know that I was there next to him when he declared his Lord accountable for everything that happened. He made Him responsible for everything."

Everyone saw that Adam was fidgeting, that he would have liked to interject something, but Eve did not give him an opportunity.

"I agreed with Adam on many things, but hearing this from his mouth I was worried that, having lost his son, he had also lost his mind. Allow me to confess truthfully to you, and to my son, that during those days the pain of losing you had not come upon me yet. I was all-consumed with Adam's wound. He was completely dependent on me. I remembered from our childhood how frightening fever can be and what our Lord said as well: if we did not drink His concoctions, more bitter than bile, death would find us. The way He described it was as if death was always present. I could not allow death to take the one and only who remained for me, and I asked for our Lord's help.

"Our Lord had me prepare some potions. He made Adam drink from some. With others He cleaned Adam's wound. For three days He hardly ate or slept, but kept His hands on Adam's chest and tracked his labored breathing and heartbeat, even when he drifted off to sleep.

"He stayed with us for weeks, even after Adam's fever diminished but he still was not strong enough to stand. At those times, his Lord conversed with him at length.

"Believe it or not, in an amazing manner, our Lord shed His skin to become human. I say this mostly to Adam, as you all know how he is. Adam sees his Lord as godlike, as a Provident Father..."

At this point Adam suddenly came to life, fuming: "Provident Father? I am eternally happy that I will see my son and his family, but these Nódians have been here just three days and they have talked your head full, Eve. You have forgotten that we are our Lord's creations; that He created us from the dust of the earth."

"I never said, nor am I saying now, that we are not of the dust of the earth. We now eat the flesh of animals, but they have grown from the vegetation of the fields. Your Lord spoke the truth when He said all life stems from the dust of the earth. It is not His fault that you understand more from His words than He states in them. It is like those with which He sent Cain away. You have spoken of exile ever since then, even though you acknowledge that it is better that our son did not stay with us but sought his own Eve elsewhere. And now we can see what a perfect Eve he has found for himself."

"Mother, tell me, did Matúzs really send me on my way with that intent?" asked Cain eagerly.

"Ask our Lord, my son," suggested Eve. "I have heard from your father that you won our Lord's protection before He sent you on your journey."

"By rejecting His curse you opposed your Lord and thereby convinced Him that you had the strength and courage to undertake the long journey," agreed Adam.

"Kió did the same thing," commented Cain, humbly.

Kió spoke up: "I knew where I was going and had reason to believe that the object of my journey was attainable. And I had somewhere to return to. Your test, which led to overcoming your fears and doubts to win Mahal, was not hidden in the length of your journey but in its uncertainty. Uncertainty can only be conquered by the will, faith, and unwavering hope within you; by not giving in to the temptation to accept a lesser mate."

"Are you thinking of the little monkey?" smiled Eve.

"So, Mahal has told you about the little animal that displayed such great interest in me. What you heard, Mother, illustrates the Nódian ability for storytelling. Mahal and I have performed this story many times and always embellished it through the strength of our imaginations."

"If this is the case," burst out Adam, "how can we know what is true in what a Nódian says and what is not? What took place and what did not?"

"Fiction can be truer than reality, we Nódians believe," said their Grand Dame. "We listen to stories every night about the same thing not because we wish to understand more about what happened but because, through the colorful tapestry of words, we gain entry into the imaginary world of the storyteller and as a result we can learn more about not only the storyteller but also ourselves."

Mahanna might have said more about the value of stories had not a guardsman arrived running. He would have wished to call her away but after he said a few words to her she pulled him next to herself and looked at Adam.

"It appears to me that you have more to say, Adam. We are listening."

"It seems you hold everything to be true and perfect that takes place in Nód and consider improper everything that refers to how other people live. Even if we cannot consider my small family a nation, our Lord's intent for us is that our progeny should populate the world. However, if what you say is true and not merely a story, that there are all sorts of peoples living elsewhere, how can this take place? Are we going to be like the animals who fight each other for their hunting ground? Is this perhaps why my Lord wanted to teach me the art of weaponry? But why didn't He say that there are people living in other worlds?"

"But, Father, you believed so!" shouted Cain. "Didn't you say when you set me on my journey that you expected me back here in the Outerworld when I found an Eve suited to me? How could you have said that if you didn't believe there are people living in other places?"

"I spoke of *one* Eve, the way there was *one* Eve in our world. So, I could think that there is *one* world somewhere else in which *one* Eve lives who our Lord intended for you if you could overcome the trial He set before you. That is what our Lord said when He comforted me while I was worried about you in my fever. Wasn't it so, Eve?"

"Your Lord said many things at that time. You only remember what you want to remember. Perhaps even now, when you see so many people here, you still wish to believe that you are the only created man in the world."

"That is what our Lord taught us! His ire will strike me down if…"

"Don't believe that, Father!" cried Cain again, surprising everyone with the force of his voice. "Or perhaps you don't remember? Your Lord was about to strike me down in His rage; but when I stood up to Him, not allowing Him to condemn me—true, I could do so easily because I had nothing to lose—His enormous rage left Him. He gave me the protection of His sign and the opportunity to start a new life in the land of Nód. You too can count on His good will if you cause Him to understand that you have the strength to take the journey of self-discovery."

Adam spoke: "I am walking my own path here in my Outerworld, which, according to the will of my Lord, I rule over."

"According to the will of your Lord, you say! But what would happen if it were revealed that He is a human like you, Adam?" asked Mahanna, looking to Eve for agreement.

After what seemed an endless silence Adam responded: "Even then He would remain the Lord of the Garden, and I would remain lord of the Outerworld."

Mahanna heard in Adam's voice that he was ready to accept the humanity of his Lord. She stood up, therefore, and said loudly so everyone could hear: "Our man who just came to me," pointing to Hardhara, the chief guardsman, "brought the news that Matúzs has already come from his island to see us but will only stand before us if we do not receive him as he once was but as he has become. I assume by this he means that he has been freed from his demons and expects us not to hold him responsible for having kidnapped the children. I recommend that we accept his condition."

"This Matúzs again!" said Adam, impatiently. "It is possible that hunting has made my ears sharper than you can imagine. You think I don't hear what you are whispering behind my back about this Matúzs, and how you could persuade me to return with you to Nód. This 'return' *back* is the most difficult part. Perhaps I still do not understand completely, unless it is that I should accept Markara as my father. But what kind of father is it that would take me by force to that Nód about which I know only what very little I have heard from you. The answer to my questions is repeatedly only 'wait, Adam, soon everything will come to light.' Furthermore, 'back to'! What else could this mean but that I got here from there. But how? You say nothing about this, not even behind my back. Not even to my woman. Eve, did you always know this?"

"I know from the Nódians that I am one year older than you. This is why I could remember times before you knew your mind. With the birth of my children certain memories surfaced, that I too had a mother who took me to her bosom. At those times I felt the soft warmth of her breasts."

"And perhaps you know who this Matúzs is that they mention so often?" asked Adam. "I must know who is waiting to speak to us."

"For some twenty years, ever since Kió first came to us, I have been wanting to understand why he called our Lord thus. From where could he have known Him before he came into our garden?"

"We cannot understand that which we are not ready to understand," said the Grand Dame.

"I am ready to understand everything about which so far I have always just heard 'It is better for you, Adam, if you learn all of this from the mouth of your Lord.'"

"And I can only say the same thing now," said Mahanna, almost apologetically. "With us slander is considered such a great offense that if possible we give the one transgressing against us the opportunity to explain his deeds himself. What we should have told you is something you would have considered slanderous against your Lord. The question is, Adam, are you prepared to ask your Lord what until now you have been asking us?"

"I am always prepared to talk with Him," retorted the lord of the Outerworld.

"Then let us not keep Matúzs, Lord of the Garden, waiting any longer! Call him here!" said Mahanna, looking to the guardsman.

"You would send a guardsman for our Lord?" asked Adam angrily.

"Perhaps we may see your Lord today who took care of you with such patience and spoke to me with such understanding when we kept vigil next to you." Eve's voice reflected a seemingly childish enthusiasm. "May I go for him?" she asked Mahanna.

"Take Cain with you. But you," she addressed the guard, "stay behind once you have shown them where Matúzs is hiding."

"Wait!" Adam called out to them. "If I understand correctly everything I have heard so far, I must be the one to get my Lord. You have often been at odds with Him, Eve, and you too, Cain. And not long ago you faced His cherub with its flaming broadsword, your greatest fear. Now it's my turn!"

"Cikara is with him too, I imagine," commented the Great Dame.

"I don't know who she is although I have heard her name many times, but I will bring her here. For years, questions have been prowling around inside me which have only come together for me now, listening to you."

EIGHTEEN

"Do you believe Matúzs will admit to Adam who he actually is? Especially to Adam, without whom his *Great Plan* would collapse?" Markara's deriding words were cut short by Eve's vigorously raised voice:

"Better if you don't speak in front of your son about his Lord this way, if you do not want to lose him forever. What can you know about His plans?"

"We heard his words enough in Nód, fomenting rebellion against the Grand Dames. Perhaps I would castigate him less if he would have actually made my son the founder of the new world of male dominion, or its leader. But there is no chance of that now."

"According to your son's belief, whatever his Lord's plan is, it will take place; if not, we try in vain to make it happen. It's possible He really wished to raise Adam to be the leader of the impending world of male dominion. There was a time when He wished to chisel a warrior out of him, without much success," said Eve, thinking how much more she preferred talking about all of this with Mahanna instead of the constantly argumentative Markara.

"We talked about this," said Mahanna. "No matter the outcome of our journey, I must fulfill the commission entrusted to me: I must find out what Matúzs' objective was in kidnapping you two."

"Does He know this?" asked Eve, pulling the Grand Dame aside and whispering in her ear so the others wouldn't hear. "I was concerned that, fearing your power, He might have wanted to have Adam kill your guardsmen."

"Only our guardsmen?" asked Mahanna in surprise. "Didn't his command, that you were to pass on to your husband, say to lead us all into the swamp?"

"It's true, that's what I said. But after I told you the story of the benevolent Matúzs fighting for my man's life I came to the realization that, even in the heat of His rage, He could not have thought to have my relatives come to see me and then be drowned in the swamp."

"What, then?"

"Obviously, He planned that, when you were overcome with hunger and thirst, Adam would save you, leaving only the guardsmen to their fate."

"You are a true Nódian, my girl. There is no greater virtue than assuming good intent on the part of one who has committed many misdeeds."

Eve then talked at length about Matúzs' healing goodness, until Markara again expressed his concern, emphatically mentioning Matúzs' magic. He did not explicitly say that the Nód Virgin fell victim to it, but it was implied. For Eve, Cikara's absence raised another issue: "Your priestess may be beautiful and kind, as you say, and her skills may be amazing, but is it more important for your Cikara to spin a web around the Lord of the Garden than to free my man from his imprisonment?"

"You're not jealous, are you, Eve?" asked Kihara in surprise, or rather more out of curiosity. Then, with a sigh, he quoted an old Nód saying: "Oh, you women! It is easier to read the thoughts of a camel with its eyes shut tight in a sandstorm than it is to read a woman's mind when her eyes are wide open looking at you."

Mahanna looked at him disapprovingly. "Don't you see that Eve wants to allow us entry into her world of questions and feelings, which, since our arrival, has been in great upheaval? You men expect us to read your minds—how to please you, answer your unvoiced questions—but when we give voice to what troubles our hearts you assume our words have a hidden meaning. You cannot tolerate that our thoughts go beyond adoring you. I did not expect this from you, Kihara."

"Forgive me, my lady. I don't know why I came forward with this. I too am concerned about Cikara."

A cry interrupted Kihara's thought. "Here they come!" Cikara stepped out of the forest together with Matúzs and Adam, who kept the priestess between them such that the hands of the two men rested on each other's shoulders.

"It is the first time Adam has touched his Lord, except when, as a child, he would sometimes raise His hand to his forehead," said Eve, surprised. "You are right, Mahanna, Cikara is truly capable of miracles."

Amid joyful upheaval and sighs of relief, only Markara commented bitterly to his wife: "I had hoped our priestess would be able to bring my son back to me. Instead, she takes him from you. Perhaps she will be a better mother to him than Matúzs was a father."

"Let us rejoice if Matúzs finds tranquility in his old age through Cikara and gives up his male-dominion mania," said Markara's wife, taking him by the arm to placate him, but Markara broke free and hurried toward those approaching from the forest while calling Kió to him.

"We must be cautious with Matúzs. I have reason to believe he is preparing for something," he said excitedly. Later, when Kió withstood his gaze without the slightest sign of concern, he added, "If we allow him to speak, he'll sway the majority of our guards to his side. You know, Kió, how convincing he can be."

"You also know, Markara—you were among his most enthusiastic followers. On that troubled night you stood up to Matúzs for the sake of your son. If you have another opportunity to do it, Adam will proudly acknowledge you as his father."

"You followed me and spied on me?"

"We followed you for your own protection."

"But then you have to know how dangerous and obsessed Matúzs is. I have a right to take my son home to Nód!"

"You know the decision of the Elders. At most we can bring him and Eve back by force only if their lives are in danger here. Leave me in peace, Markara. I'm going ahead to greet them."

"If necessary, I will confront Matúzs by myself! Even if by then Cikara considers my son to be hers."

"Until now you were concerned that Matúzs held your son under his power as some kind of god. But now it is as if you are even more concerned that, recognizing him as a human, Adam will continue to be attached to his guardian father. Your fear for your son has made you lose your mind, Markara. Return to your woman or I'll have you taken back by the guardsmen."

Kió hurried to warn Matúzs of Adam's natural father having lost his mind.

Markara felt it was his last chance to get the others on his side, and he was dismayed when he saw the joyous smile with which Eve beheld the woman and two men conjoined.

"See, this can only mean that Adam finally looks on his Lord as human," she said happily.

"But you don't know that it was as a human that he confounded many of us in Nód. We should not have allowed our son to talk with him alone!"

"What has come over you, Markara?" Eve smiled at him. "Do you want to get him back as your son? Yes? Then don't try to tear him away from the father who raised him and who will shortly arrive here with him."

"Raised him?" Markara snapped. "He kidnapped him! Do you understand the word, Eve? Kidnapped!"

"I understand the word but I know it does not mean the same thing to Adam as it does to you. He does not remember you as his parents, even to the extent that I do. I have known for days who among you is my birth mother, although I have not been able to talk to her as my mother or embrace her."

"That's your problem!"

"Don't forget the Nódian saying," said the Grand Dame, raising her voice. "'The more people your love flows to, the more everyone receives.' It is the same with hatred. You can turn your son against Matúzs with your accusatory words, but you won't win his filial love as a result. If you persist in this way, he may turn away from you forever."

"While he saw himself as the servant of his Lord who he considered to be his creator, I could accept that explanation for his behavior. But I cannot permit that from now on. Having recognized Matúzs as human, he serves him as his son. You should have told him who his real father was before letting him go to Matúzs."

"He wanted to go to his Lord!" retorted Eve. "You could not forbid him to do that."

"I am not returning to Nód without my only son, now that I have finally found him. And of course, I am taking Seth with me too; after all, he is my grandchild. If, Eve, you wish to stay, that's your affair. Discuss it with your own parents."

"I would be pleased to go to Nód. I get along with all of you. I don't consider myself different or less than you. And it is a great joy for me to talk with other women at last. Not so, Adam. He cannot abide so many people together all at once. Perhaps he would never get used to so many. Adam probably went to his Lord just now because he would not have been able to speak to Him in front of so many people. And if he were to hear such things as you have said, you can be sure we would not see him for weeks."

"Don't worry," said the Grand Dame, touching Eve's arm. "We won't let Markara ruin everything we have so carefully arranged. Adam's father's right extends only so far as trying to convince you to follow him to Nód *voluntarily*."

"There are other ways for you to be together with your son and grandson," smiled Eve at Markara again. "Why don't you stay with us as our dear relative?"

"Would this be possible?" asked Markara in a voice that changed from one moment to the next, as does someone's who did not believe his ears. "But why not?" he cried out joyfully. "After all, I am not tied to Nód by close relatives. My woman's only grandchildren are here, with whom she is joyfully playing even now."

"You see, it is true that words of love open every heart, finding a solution to everything."

"I'll go fetch my woman." Markara turned toward the field but then, as if his heart had missed a beat, he stopped. He noticed Kió hardly half a stone's throw away, followed by Cikara and Matúzs.

"But where is my son?" he yelled, frightened.

"Don't be afraid! I am not the same as the one you encountered in the darkness of night," said Matúzs to calm him. "Your son is waiting for your paternal embrace at the same forest clearing."

"Take your woman with you," added Cikara. "So that Adam can also embrace his birth mother."

"She's with her grandchildren. Send her after me!" Makara said, turning from them. "I am hurrying to my son."

Cikara and Matúzs looked at each other, smiling. They knew he wanted to hide his tears of joy from them.

NINETEEN

When they arrived at the camp everyone greeted Matúzs at length. Then they questioned Cikara. Was she frightened of the incandescent pair of eyes? Did she know that Matúzs was behind it? Is she happy now with Matúzs? How do they envision their new lives? And, of course, they supplied the couple with wishes of goodwill. Eve discovered in Matuzs' glowing face the same goodness she last saw in him when she was nursing Adam, and could not stop praising the priestess's amazing powers that had brought back the former Matúzs.

"I merely did what my office required and my heart dictated," said Cikara. "The amazing one is you, Eve. The love radiating from your eyes and the strength shining from your body confirm all that I heard about you from Kió and your son."

Mahanna interjected: "We recognize in you the Matúzs thought to have been lost forever, who we remembered as our beloved master teacher; we hold your every word to be so important that we would like Adam and Markara to hear them as well." Matúzs nodded in agreement, then turned to Cain.

"Cikara told the story of what a perfect woman you found for yourself, son. I imagine that is her with the children in her arms. I would embrace her." Cain did not even have to nod; Mahal was already running toward him.

"I have heard so much good and bad about you, but I feel you have left the bad behind. Thank you for having sent Cain to me; I could not have imagined a better husband. And look what beautiful children he sired for me!" The happy husband was already approaching, his smaller son on his shoulder. Seth was coaxing tongue-tied Hánokh toward Matúzs; he put his hands to his forehead so Matúzs could not wipe his tear-filled eyes when he embraced him.

Cikara then introduced all the Nódians to Matúzs one by one.

"You two have already met," she pointed to Kió. "We can thank him that we are here. He is the one who was of the opinion that you allowed Cain to come to us as a sign of life about yourself and the innocents…" The priestess's words trailed off because she realized they required explanation. She took Matúzs' hand and told him how Kió had taken upon himself the weight of Matúzs' exile by the elders because he had only disclosed the whereabouts of the kidnapped after so many years.

"He related all this in defense of Cain, in order to prove

that he is actually a son of Nód. Kió knew that after his long journey the boy would die if we did not accept him. Remember, Matúzs, I've already told you that you must forgive your once favorite pupil for having violated his oath to you."

Matúzs motioned to Kió to come to him. As a sign of his forgiveness, Matúzs kissed Kió on the forehead. Then, to the joy of everyone, they recounted their last meeting. Of course there were elements that Matúzs remembered differently from how Kió had described that meeting to the Nódians. Meanwhile, Adam had arrived with his father, and mostly gave credence to Matúzs, while Eve almost always supported Kió. Mahanna thought it best if she interjected.

"Certainly what transpired did not take place in two different ways. We can believe that you, Matúzs, were in fact ready to allow your wards to leave, and we know that without Kió's intercession it would have been difficult for you to pronounce the words of dismissal to them. What is important is that you allowed them, nonetheless, to leave with your blessing, and so did not burden their new life with a sense of guilt. We can return to all this, but before that, let Adam have a word. Cikara indicated that between you, Matúzs, and Adam, everything that is important about who wants to live how and where has already been said. Eve has spoken about this. No matter what you decide, Adam, she will stay with you, and we respect your decisions."

"I have been working on a good-sized cave for many years, the mouth of which was so narrow that I would never have discovered it had it not swallowed those rare white foxes that I had been tracking for days. I made it comfortable in every way for you, son," said Adam, smiling at Cain, "so you and your woman would have a place to live. I did this because I always believed that you would return one day. But I have now heard from Cikara how happy you are with your Mahal in Nód. So, I only ask that you come to see us whenever you wish. This is how I get to where I should have begun: I heard from Markara, my father… please don't take offense, but it will be difficult for me to get used to the joyful realization that I have relatives! As I was saying, Eve asked you to stay with us, and to our great delight you have accepted. So, I would offer that very comfortable cave to you, which is not far from here, so your grandchildren can come to visit anytime. Do you agree, Eve?"

"It will be good to know your parents are near us—especially your mother, because a few days ago I felt that a new life was beginning to move inside me," said Eve, snuggling up to her man. "Also, Cikara, the way I see you looking at Matúzs, you have no other desire than to present him with the child for which he yearned. Is it so, Matúzs?"

"I loved you both as my own children, but I must admit there were times when I longed for the fruit of my own loins."

The conversation, interwoven with joyful and fanciful daydreams, went on for some time; but later, during their evening meal, Kió was able to sit next to Matúzs so he could put to him the questions to which he had been searching for answers since hearing so much from Cain about his parents' Outerworld life.

"I know you kept your promise that when you let your wards leave your Garden you would give them everything they needed for their new life. I did see that they took with them two bundles each, which likely contained those fine leather clothes you promised them."

"When I first saw Adam daydreaming about the Outerworld on the mountain protecting the Gihon strait," answered Matúzs, "I started to cut warm clothes for them. I knew that sooner or later I had to let them go into the freedom of the world, where the nights are colder in the open fields and the wind is more biting. Of course, I also gave them warm homespuns for nighttime blankets. If only I had the strength to let them go sooner! The more I delayed it the harsher our disagreements became, and I did not want us to part in anger. I owe you my thanks, Kió, because through your intercession I could dismiss my wards peacefully."

Kió would have liked to continue listening to Matúzs' heartfelt words, just the two of them, but the others overheard what they were talking about and quietly gathered around them. They allowed Kió to ask further: "In fact, I wanted to ask you about this, Matúzs. You could have purchased not only homespun fabrics in exchange for the ambers you found in your Garden, but also many other things that would have made working the earth and hunting easier. You could have hidden lances, shovels, and hoes in their bundles. We know from Cain that his parents never had such things. Why didn't you want to make their work easier? Was it perhaps because of your curse?"

"I only wished to caution you," said Matúzs, turning to Adam and Eve, "that hard work awaited you in the uncultivated land beyond my Garden. If, in my shock and rage prompted by your opposition, it came out of my mouth as a curse, as Cikara says, I am sorry. Do not remember me as someone who had no control over his tongue when his demons took charge of him, but as someone who has given over to his wards all his knowledge so that at least a vestige of the wisdom acquired in Nód would remain, should the Eastern empires sweep our city off the face of the earth. I also had to prepare Adam and Eve to be the only Nódians remaining alive once those overcoming your city put all its residents to the sword. That is why I gave them the knowledge that is more valuable than anything, the power of love, which made Nód richer than all its neighboring people. But how could they have remained alive in the Outerworld if hostile people lived all around? Only if they were capable of providing everything for themselves."

"I understand your objective now," answered Kió, "and I admit that you have reached it. We recognized the amazing knowledge and wisdom in Cain that his parents had transmitted to him. You meted out a weighty burden on them but they lacked nothing. The question now is whether, despite our arrival, what you so skillfully planned can continue."

"You can always build a better house on a good foundation than the original plan. But I must admit, Cikara and I have already discussed all this. I am proud that this wise woman, and you as well, Kió, were my students. In the past few days I have often thought about what my life would have been like had I remained Nód's teacher after Cikara and I fell in love. But she does not wish to speak about this. It is only important, she says, that we have found each other now and Cikara is pregnant."

"I hope you see, Matúzs, that we are on a good path to fulfilling your command to 'multiply,'" said Eve.

"My command?" Matúzs looked at Eve in surprise. "I made no such 'commandment.' How many misunderstandings there must be between us! Not only my irate words, which were thought of as curses. I see now that you considered my counsel, my directives prompted by worry, to be commandments, and that you took my protective forewarnings to be prohibitions. It was not my commandment 'to multiply'; after all, every living creature multiplies from an inner compulsion. My observation was that people should multiply vastly in all directions and increasingly inhabit fertile lands. The older Nódians have all heard this before."

"Too often at that," commented Biko-ma, the doula, who in the last few days had become even more reticent than usual. There was serious reason for her restraint. She had not told Mahal yet that she suspected she was carrying twins beneath her heart. It was only after that morning, when she thoroughly palpated the expectant mother's belly, that she shared her supposition with Cain.

"If I were you I would not tell Mahal yet; she would be very disappointed if the news did not prove to be true, and I cannot be entirely certain of it. But it is better that you know, since you have to decide how long we stay here," she concluded, although she hoped that Cain would soon talk about returning. However, the conversation did not take that direction; rather, Matúzs wanted at all costs to clarify his earlier intentions.

"I traveled some time ago in various worlds…" Matúzs started in his storytelling voice, but Cikara stopped him: "Don't you see that these good people have already forgiven you your past? Instead, talk about how you see Nód's future, and that of your wards. There are very many paths leading to the future. Which one should we take?"

"I will tell you, but what is this great hurry? I would like you to know what has been causing me heartache all these years. I hope I will have time for everything; after all, you may be delayed for weeks until the ebbing of the rivers allows for safe passage."

"Tell us about everything, Matúzs, but let me say the stakes are not small. The elders have authorized me," proclaimed Mahanna in an official voice, "to revoke your exile if I am convinced that you will never more endanger Nód's peacefulness. For this we must know: What was your objective with the ones you took from us?"

"Well, let us begin with my wanting to raise Nód's first king from the boy child," said Matúzs. "A strong-armed and just king such as Ithuriszk's young leader Dammetra, the likes of whom I have not encountered anywhere in the course of my travels. But Adam preferred to walk the forests with me rather than listen to my teachings. Eve was much more inclined to listen and ask questions all day long. I had to concede that I could sculpt a queen from Eve sooner than a woman for her king. Their minds work quite differently, as you may have already discovered. Eve compounds her already acquired knowledge with questions and reaches the answers on her own. Her woman's knowledge is like the woven fabric that shields those who are hers from the chill of the bleak night. She is the mother wolf ready for anything and does everything for those who are her own. She has never opposed me for herself but only for Adam, who for a long time she felt to be more her son than her brother, and only in the last few years her mate. Adam, on the other hand, is the wolf father, who is only interested in knowledge that helps him provide for his family: how to follow the tracks of beasts and trap the evening meal. At first I did not mind this. I believed it would help him as a warrior. But I was a complete failure at this; how could he have possibly imagined why I wanted to teach him the use of weapons when I could not confess to him that there are a multitude of people living in the worlds beyond the Outerworld and, among them, those capable of all manner of evil? By the time I got to tell Adam he was not the first and only human, which, based on the stories he heard from me in his childhood, he believed himself to be, it was too late. And I did not have the courage to deprive him of this belief, which I thought to be the single thread that tied him to me. Cikara encouraged me to get over this. She said that Adam should rather regard me as some sort of grandfather. And because you too, Markara, at one time, if you remember, thought of me as your father."

"Tell us, Matúzs, how you see the future of your wards now. Would you permit them to return with us, and, if so, would you expect Adam to form a warrior nation from Nód?"

"I had to concede a long time ago that I could not count on that. I saw that Adam and Eve only knew one human relationship, that of love. Good warriors are not made of this. So I had to rethink everything. The new plan may prove to be good because Adam still maintains that they consider this Outerworld their home. They would go to Nód only to visit; later, perhaps. This made me very happy because now I see the future of these two worlds woven together, especially as Cikara has confirmed the reports that have concerned me half my life. The distant warlike nations have, at the cost of bloody wars, already formed into empires. The people of Nód could not withstand their armies. It is better, therefore, if Nód remains a peaceful nation. If those armies threaten Nód and you receive news of this, come here, where we are protected by the floods of the Euphrates and Gihon and from the west by the impassable swamp of the Ai."

Matúzs' unexpected offer was followed by a lengthy debate. First, he was asked how reliable his current information was on the warlike Eastern empires.

"Before I left Nód some thirty years ago, I thought it was urgent that we raise a generation of warriors. You have no time for that now. However, a few years is enough for you to get used to the idea that Nód is not a place but a nation that can be Nód elsewhere too. Only don't wait until your enemies are at the gates of your city before you pack up your belongings and come here!"

The assembled discussed the innumerable difficulties of moving the entire Nódian nation to the Outerworld. The fire, which had been restoked several times, was dying down again when Mahanna spoke, in a raised voice so the men on the other side of the fire who were already discussing how many burden-bearing camels and donkeys they would need could also hear.

"Just one more thing, Matúzs," she said. "Perhaps I should wait with this but as we have come this far let me say without mincing words that in order for the people of Nód to win back their trust in you and accept your offer, we must account for what so far we have not come to know; that is, what brought on your desperate outbursts?"

When Matúzs looked at her uncomprehendingly, Mahanna added: "We are thrilled to see that Cikara has exorcised your demons, but we know there are demons that are capable of returning. We would be comforted if we knew more about your obsession, your demons, so we could rest assured of no longer having to fear them."

"I am happy to tell you this before we retire for the night."

Matúzs waited until the crackling of the dry twigs with

which Adam had once again brought the campfire to life died down. Staring into the flames he said:

"I saw, while still in Nód, the future emerging from the past. In the dark of night, the earth was barren; emptiness filled everything. Then, in the warming light of the rising sun, the world burst into bloom. Soon, hardworking people appeared and life proceeded in peace. The springtime landscape was alive with birdsong and the laughter of children as the sun rose higher in its course. This was the prolific era of growing in numbers, when giving life was of utmost importance. Nations were ruled by Eves. Later, when people populated all the habitable land, they turned against each other. I saw an unavoidable future of envy and strife, of bitter arguments over fruitful lands and wells with good water. The clubs and lances, used until then only against animals, were turned into weapons by the more aggressive nations. Women no longer gave birth to populate the earth but to replace the many thousands killed in wars.

"I didn't understand how the mountains of corpses could grow so big, but then I saw the monsters. They were vomiting rocks, followed by fire-breathers. They rule the earth and sky; they even burst forth from the seas. Nothing sets a limit to the assault of human cruelty. I saw with horror mankind's progeny hiding in these monsters as they battled each other. They had no regard for anything or anyone, not even women and children. Destruction and death followed them everywhere. The sky was covered by stinking black smoke. By the time the sun reached high noon the gods couldn't even see the earth's misery.

"I saw Adam's offspring everywhere among the dead. The destroyed cities were rebuilt by other Adams, and then destroyed again. These images are horrific, dreadful, but not difficult to comprehend. In my most tormented dreams this is how the world appeared to me, and in that awareness I taught that we must not be surpassed in combativeness by other nations. We must prepare. The time will come when we will have to defend ourselves against those who are capable of giving their life for a foothold on the land. Only armed nations can survive this conflict. The victors triumph over other nations, combine with them to conquer more nations, until a single empire comes into being and then there is eternal peace.

"However, to my great disappointment, the course of my apparitions later showed that the struggle of nations does not end even after the long succession of generations. Their dragons give birth to even more destructive dragons, empires are built and fall into ruin again and again. This had for many years nearly driven me insane because it was not for such eternal conflict that I wanted to raise Adam to be Nód's wise king.

"My apparitions tortured me for years because I wanted to see that man's dominion leads to the empire of peacefulness. Then, at dawn today, in Cikara's embrace, I came to discover with unbelievable relief the arrival of reconciliation. But I did not see any Adams in this. They were not the ones to bring about resolution. Who, then? And suddenly Eve appeared before me. Eve who did not accept my curse, my warning, that her desire would cause her to be forever under her husband's domination.

"It was only after Cikara opened my eyes that the meaning of the young Adam and Eve leaving my island for the Outerworld unfolded before me. Until then I thought it was only the hazy vision of my tearing eyes that caused them to merge into one as they receded into the distance. Now, at last, I understand: it is the culminating wisdom of my days of apparition that after the greed-driven wars of nations have failed to define the future, an Adam and an Eve, no longer a brother and sister under my control but rather a self-reliant Man and Woman, will merge into one in a transformative union. Eve's sons will accept the Eve living inside each of them and create a future in which strength and gentleness, man and woman, will rule in the name of love."

EPILOGUE

THE PEOPLE OF the Outerworld gradually multiplied. Families dreaming of more fertile agricultural land moved there from Nód, having heard of unplowed fields, fruit-bearing trees. With time there were those who journeyed to Nód from the Outerworld, including Seth, Adam and Eve's son, who also found his woman there. Eve's first daughter, who was much admired for her beauty, was given the name Neha and found her man in a family that arrived from Nód. Soon a good-sized city developed in the Outerworld, which Adam and Eve never left. Matúzs, on the other hand, having had enough of life, asked his woman, Cikara, to take him to Nód so that he could die there. By that time Mahal had risen to be the youngest among Nód's Grand Dames. As a result, she was the one who, at the news of Matúzs and Cikara's arrival, hurried ahead to greet them, with Cain by her side. That is how they proceeded into the city, to the enthusiastic joy of its residents.

Matúzs had lived two full moons in Nód when news of the Ithuriszk Empire's powerful army, fast approaching from the direction of sunrise, reached the city. Many felt Matúzs had sensed the oncoming danger and returned to help the Nódians prepare for their massive migration. In exchange for the many handfuls of amber brought from the island they were able to acquire several hundred swift camels from the nomads. They were able to take with them not only all Nódians from the little ones to the elderly, but all of their valuables—their looms, potter's wheels, and blacksmith's forge. They made Cain leader of the journey; Kió and Kihara had already left the company of the living. Matúzs did not return to his Eden island with them. At dawn on the day of their departure, a great sadness and exhaustion came over him, having saved his beloved people through his prescience and persistence. Cikara took her beloved man into her lap with the comforting and transporting words of the Nód Virgins' poems for the dead. She caressed and stroked his white hair until Matúzs drifted off. In his last moments, however, he saw with his spiritual eye that every one of his people crossed the Euphrates, and later the Gihon too.

Ithuriszk's King Dammetra did not follow the plentiful tracks left by the fleeing multitude. He even called back his marauding advance guard, as he was so frightened by what welcomed him in the temple of sacred Hunán. His bodyguards had reported that they found not a single living soul in the entire city of Nód, only one deceased woman and a man in their temple, whose bodies were not decayed by death. The horror of his toughest soldiers frightened

Dammetra. He placed guards around the temple so that the mercenaries, terrified of magic, would not be able to enter. Then he stepped inside the temple alone and bravely approached the altar stone, where he found the body of the woman in whose lap the man lay. Based on everything he had heard, he recognized in them the legendary Matúzs and Cikara. He was ready to leave when the priestess's eyes opened. Dammetra, who had never retreated from anything, lost his nerve when he clearly heard a voice: "Do not harm our people!" Then and there, in front of Hunán's altar, he swore an oath that he kept his entire life.

According to Ithuriszk custom, the two bodies were burned on a huge pyre in order to free their spirits to enrich the primal mist floating above all, giving life to everything.

After the newly arrived Nódians merged with those in the Outerworld they anointed Eve among the Grand Dames, but those who saw her appear before the Nódian emissaries years before continued to see a queen in her. Slowly everyone came to the belief that, in contrast to the Ithuriszk king, they should have a queen. Eve, however, replied to their invitation in this manner: "Because my entire life I did not accept Adam's domination over me I cannot rule over him in our old age. Make your journey's successful leader, my firstborn son, your king, and his woman, the kind and wise Mahal, your queen." Nód's united people in the Outerworld joyfully accepted this because they understood that in those two strength and gentleness, mind and heart, would rule together.

Among the progeny of Nód's first king and queen were numerous perfect women-men and men-women similar to them who traversed the world while awaiting the arrival of their time. After the migration that stripped everyone of their roots, however, dissension spread in the Outerworld. This was caused by bad blood among good neighbors in Nód that arose when one of them believed his partner had acquired better agricultural land at the boundary of Gihon. There were those who took the remedy for their grievance into their own hands. One thought to light a fire to destroy the farming partner's grain fields that produced a better crop than his, but, as soon as the tip of the fire-starter rod began to smolder, a tongue of flame burst forth from a heap of rocks behind him and purified his heart.

Eve recognized that the white magic emanated from the rocks she had piled up long ago to close off the mouth of the cave in which she and Adam had placed her second-born son Abel's dead body. Many then made pilgrimage to the cave in the belief that Abel, who became a victim of his own malice, would redeem them from their wickedness. Eve was comforted that in his death her short-lived son was doing some good, and indeed after a few generations all recollection of the boy's patricidal intent lapsed into oblivion. Nor in the course of many generations did Cain's name remain alive as the kind and just first king of the Nódians. Mahal's name, also, was completely forgotten.

But it was not merely the all-pervasive sand shrouding the ages that distorted an accurate accounting of what truly happened. All the apparitions that tormented Matúzs came to pass. The Ithurisz Empire that peacefully assimilated Nód was conquered by another empire, and that by another. Ark builders arrived for whom the Gihon's flooding represented no obstacle. They took every descendant of Nód into servitude, and the memories they maintained in stories passed down by word of mouth gradually became corrupted. Chroniclers of those in power rewrote Nód's ancient stories in such a way as to assert the superiority of God-given male domination. Violence, stemming for the most part from envy and greed, became a daily occurrence. Ultimately, thousands upon thousands of brothers died at the hands of their brothers. Mankind could be seen as waiting anxiously for some sign of more gentle times, like a subterranean brook bursting forth to the surface.

AFTERWORD

East of Eden

The counter-story of the people of Nód

by Ágnes Heller

THE BIBLE PROVIDES inexhaustible material for a novelist. There is a good deal of text in the Holy Scripture itself that we may read as a novel, such as Jacob's and Joseph's stories. Writers with less genius than Thomas Mann do not even attempt to compete with these texts. The many Jesus and Moses novels create the tribulations of their heroes during the years that did not merit mention in the Bible. What happened to Moses from the time the pharaoh's daughter found him up until he killed the slave driver? How did Jesus live after the Jews fled to Egypt and until the beginning of his mission? Where text is missing, the imagination can soar freely.

These days, among other reasons because of the effect of feminism, the stories revolve mostly around the women players in the Bible. Books have been written about Sarah's life before and after meeting Abraham, Lila, Cipora, and Dina. In the novel about Dina the author includes the stories of all four wives of Jacob. We experience along with them their very first menstruation and we suffer and rejoice along with them during their labor pains. Such female experiences are emphasized in novels because in ancient times as well as yesterday and today they occur similarly. What develops around them is actually the story.

Laszlo Z. Bito in his first biblical novel (*The Curse of Obedience*) took the same path as the authors of Moses and Samson books. He chose Isaac as his protagonist, the ancient father about whom the Bible is rather tight-lipped. We know something of the astonishing circumstances of his birth, that his father wanted to sacrifice him, and that he married Rebecca, Laban's sister. When we next encounter him he is old, blind, dying, and has been swindled. Bito's Isaac novel fills in the voids.

But he does not try to have us understand his narrative as a reconstruction of "reality," the way similarly themed novels do. He does not insinuate that things could have happened the way his novel suggests; he does not provide a map and family tree. Furthermore, it is consciously and deliberately out of context when he puts thoughts in Isaac's mouth that were conceived in the Age of Enlightenment. The biblical Isaac becomes Laszlo Bito's elucidative mask.

Eden Revisited is partly a continuation of this tradition, but partly it advances on new paths. Let us look at the Bible. Adam and Eve, on the advice of the serpent, bite into the fruit of the tree of knowledge and henceforth make a distinction between good and evil. As punishment God curses the serpent, adding that there will be eternal enmity between Him and the woman. He does not curse the woman, merely tells her that because of her trespass she will birth her children in pain and the man will have dominion over her. He then curses the earth, that it should yield stalks, and that man will earn his bread by the sweat of his brow until he returns unto the earth from which he came. Afterward, Adam gave the name Eve (Hava), mother of all mankind, to every woman. Next comes the expulsion from Eden. Then Adam "knows" Eve and she gives birth to Cain, then Abel. There is no word about a girl child. God accepts Abel's sacrifice but not Cain's. Cain, the farmer, entices his younger brother, the shepherd, into the field where, out of jealousy, he kills him. As a result, God forces him into exile from the land of his parents but puts a sign on his forehead for protection so no one can harm him. Cain wanders for many days and winds up in the city of Nód, east of Eden.

God kept the man and his woman on a rather short leash in the Garden of Paradise. However, because they ate from the fruit of the tree of knowledge, He left them alone enough that He did not designate murder as a taboo. If human beings are capable of distinguishing between good and evil, well, let them! But humans without a leash, that is, without commandments, become the other's wolf. Violence rules the earth, children are killed. This is how long the initial story of mankind lasted, which ends with the deluge. This is the biblical story on which Laszlo Bito creates variations.

However, he does not belong in the company of those Bible critics who wish to position "real events" in place of the Bible's mythological events. He does not dispute the biblical text wearing the mask of a historian or scientist; indeed, he doesn't even regard it as mythology—except in the original Greek meaning of the word, that is, an event, a story. He is not an elucidator in the sense that he wishes to contradict a "false" event with a "true" one. Rather, he answers with a counter-story to the tale. If he regards this counter-story as being more true than the original (and he does consider it such), he does not base that judgment on his story being more "realistic." In essence, Nód as depicted by Bito is not more of a reality than the biblical story. What is more true in it for Bito is not its historical reality, but its historical message.

Of course, it is unavoidable here and there to evade the contradictions in the Bible. How could Adam and Eve have been the first human couple if God exiles their boy child to a well populated city lying east of Eden? This contradiction Bito resolves by leaving God out of the picture.

In order to avoid misunderstandings, the author does not say that Adam and Eve's guardian, the Lord of the Garden, is not God, therefore there is no God. Because of this, God could still exist. Yet, how could it be, he asks, that there is a first pair of humans while in the neighborhood there are other people living?

Bito's tale explores that contradiction. After the Lord of the Garden exiles Cain he goes off on a pilgrimage and reaches the city of Nód (also stated in the Bible). He soon learns from stories told there that a wise man named Matúzs kidnapped two babies, a boy and a girl, and took them with him to a seemingly unreachable island. These children, isolated from the world, grew up in the belief that Matúzs created them and they are the only humans on Earth.

Since Bito's counter-story here expresses the spirit of the Enlightenment, he must liberate himself from the miraculous elements of the original story. The one who tempted Adam and Eve to eat from the fruit of the tree of knowledge could not be animal, he had to be human; otherwise, how could he have been able to speak? Similarly, what does birth represent for a woman who has no idea what it actually is, who had no mother or grandmother or a woman companion who could have enlightened her?

The most important modification of the biblical text at the same time evokes the spirit of Freud. In place of the biblical Adam and Eve story, Freud proposed the story of the "ancient herd." In the beginning there was one male and one female and they had numerous sons. (It is interesting that there are no girls in Freud's story either.) The woman is possessed by the father only. The boys want to share the woman and so they kill their father. Afterward they become so frightened by their deed that they begin to worship their father's spirit as God.

Bito's story is far more human. Eve is the only woman. She allows Cain to possess her, but not Abel, who sees the cause of this in his father. For that reason he wants to kill Adam. He raises his hand against him, but Cain prevents the murder, which only succeeds at the cost of his younger brother's life. Let's not forget, he does not yet know what it is to kill another human being. Furthermore, no one has prohibited this yet (the biblical God only prohibits it for the second humanity, i.e., after the deluge).

In order to change the story in this way, something had to be said about both Abel and Cain, about whom the Bible is considerably reticent. Bito solves this problem very well. Abel, as we know, is a shepherd and Cain a farmer, according to Scripture. So what kind of human being could the first shepherd have been? Certainly not placid, peace loving, since he had to break in the wild animals, and doing that could promote cruelty and unrelenting rage. And the first farmer? Likely tame and patient. Breaking the soil does not hurt the land, so he does not acquire either rage or cruelty.

Bito's objection to the biblical story, therefore, is not that it is a tale, since his story, the counter-story, is also a tale. From one perspective, to which I shall return, it is all the more so.

Bito as a contemporary man and one-time medical researcher is primarily angered that God cursed humans with death. For my part, I interpret the novel's passages relating to this quite differently, but this is not the decisive factor here. The decisive factor is the traditional interpretation. Tradition, primarily Christian tradition, does in fact regard death as God's curse; otherwise Christ (God) would not have had to redeem mankind from death. Bito shares his outrage with thinkers of the Enlightenment, and also numerous representatives of twentieth-century existential philosophy, such as Heidegger.

But let us accompany Cain along with the author to the city of Nód.

Bito's counter-story was conceived in the style and fantasy of the spirit of the French Enlightenment. In this it resembles Voltaire's "savage man," or what Rousseau describes as the world of "noble savages," or Diderot's Bougainville experience on its distant island.

We land in a peaceful happy city, with agreeable nature and climate and even more friendly and tolerant people. There are customs and rules, but they too are people-friendly and gentle. Paradise is not indigenous to the Garden of Eden but to Nód. Behold, the world of the Golden Age. Here, it is not the only two people living in the Golden Age, one man and one woman, Adam and Eve, who have not yet achieved knowledge and are incapable of distinguishing good from bad.

While the authors of the Bible have no illusions regarding human nature, even if they do not exactly consider humankind warped, Bito's counter-story—similar to Rousseau's tale—proclaims that mankind is inherently good and noble and it is only history that made him degenerate. We can question, of course, if all this is true, what made Bito's Abel character evil? Why did he resort to patricide? Bito has an answer to this too, and the answer sheds light on the fundamental notion of Nód city's utopia.

Women rule in the city of Nód. Or rather, they don't really rule because where women lead, or let's say hold people together, there is no need for ruling. The women are benevolent, gentle, wise, givers of life.

In Bito's story the trouble begins with male dominion. In the Bible story it is when God commands Eve to obey her husband. The Bible story can continue from the beginning of male dominion. Wars, murders, and destruction can follow.

Bito's "Lord of the Garden" wants to make a warrior of Adam. That is why he kidnaps him along with Eve as babies from the peaceful city of Nód. But if the "Lord of the Garden" wanted to make Adam and his offspring into warriors, why did he not succeed in this? How is it possible for wild militaristic nations to show up from afar and in the end destroy the city of Nód and decimate the residents of Eden?

The irony in this is not foreign to the ironies of the Enlightenment, and this is the case with Bito's counter-story. Bito's Eve is an exceptional figure, courageous, passionate, full of the joys of life, a wise woman made to rule. No matter what the "Lord of the Garden" (or, if we like, God) thinks up so consequentially, Eve always remains the stronger and stays with her Adam, who is a namby-pamby fellow next to his outsize woman.

Bito's counter-story, as I have said, follows the tradition of the Enlightenment in its structure and style, and often in its content too. As "in the old order there is neither possession nor power. Men hunt but do not possess the beast," although there are instances when it is still the progeny of the Garden of Eden who set the standard: "I overlooked the nakedness so naturally worn by Eve and could not imagine her in the clothing of our women." But the counter-story is of the twenty-first century, so that Bito has to put not only yesterday's concepts into the mouths of his heroes but today's as well. For example, "we must believe in ourselves." But the prime concept cannot be found in a particular sentence, figure, or stream of thought, as it permeates the entire book. And this is a man-inspired and articulated feminism: the glorification of the female gender, although in his characters' lengthy conversations Bito emphasizes that he is not dreaming of the return of a matriarchal lifestyle. He casts his hope for a better world in the evolution of a post-patriarchal society, still in outline development.

All counter-stories are masks of the author who wants to teach something, confess something pro and con, but who does so in an intermediary capacity, as storyteller. The residents and institutions of the city of Nód are liberal: enlightened, tolerant, and supportive of minorities. Eve and the Nódians, with united force, free Adam from his batty superstitions; for example, that he believes the "Lord of the Garden," at times benevolent, at times impatient, to be his creator.

However, Bito does not relate his counter-story in order to free us from superstition. The Bible story is not superstition but, if we wish, a tale emitting a very realistic anthropology. Bito puts the following thought into the mouth of a wise woman: "A tale can be truer than reality... We gain entrance into the imaginary world of the storyteller through the colorful tapestry of words, and through them we can learn more about not only the storyteller but also ourselves." This refers to both the story and the counter-story.

The counter-story is a counter-story not because it incorporates into events our life experiences, but our ideals and desires. The counter-story is criticism of the tale; not criticism of the superstition but of merciless reality. On the Bible's palette many colors find a place. The Jewish Bible does not paint anyone white. The counter-story wishes us to see what we may possibly become, or rather, what we could have possibly been.

About Bruce Chilton

Bruce Chilton is one of the foremost scholars in the world of early Christianity and Judaism. He wrote the first critical translation of and commentary for the Aramaic version of Isaiah (*The Isaiah Targum*), as well as academic studies that analyze Jesus in his Judaic context (*A Galilean Rabbi and His Bible*; The *Temple of Jesus*; *Pure Kingdom*). His other principal publications include: *Rabbi Jesus: An Intimate Biography*; *Rabbi Paul: An Intellectual Biography*; *Mary Magdalene: A Biography*; *Resurrection Logic: How Jesus' First Followers Believed God Raised Him from the Dead*; and, most recently, *The Herods: Murder, Politics, and the Art of Succession*. He has taught in Europe at the universities of Cambridge, Sheffield, and Münster, and in the United States at Yale University (as the first Lillian Claus Professor of New Testament) and Bard College. Currently Bernard Iddings Bell Professor of Philosophy and Religion at Bard, he directs the Institute of Advanced Theology.

About Ágnes Heller

Ágnes Heller (1929–2019) was a renowned Hungarian philosopher and social critic. She was the author of numerous books on philosophy, politics, literature, and culture, including: *On Instincts*; *A Theory of History*; *The Power of Shame: A Rational Perspective*; *Eastern Left, Western Left: Totalitarianism, Freedom and Democracy* (with Ferenc Fehér); *A Philosophy of Morals*; *The Time Is Out of Joint: Shakespeare as Philosopher of History*; and *Immortal Comedy: The Comic Phenomenon in Art, Literature, and Life*. Heller was the recipient of many awards and prizes, and she was a core member of the Budapest School's philosophical forum in the 1960s. She taught political theory for twenty-five years at the New School for Social Research in New York City. Heller lived, wrote, and lectured in Budapest.

About The Institute of Advanced Theology

The Institute of Advanced Theology (IAT) at Bard College was founded in 1996 by Bruce Chilton to create the kind of genuine, critical understanding that will make real religious pluralism possible. Since its inception, IAT's work has focused on refining the newest critical research methods to pursue a comparative approach to the study of religion, exploring how religions influence history, society and one another, and are in turn influenced by them. The Institute holds lecture series, conferences, and colloquiums (www.bard.edu/iat).

About Natus Books

Natus Books, founded in 2019, is an imprint of the Institute for Publishing Arts, a 501(c)3 corporation dedicated to challenging and expanding conceptions of human possibility. The Institute is the sponsor of Station Hill Press, since 1977 the publisher of poetry, fiction, translations and non-fiction, primarily in the areas of literary philosophy and mind, body and spirit. Both Natus and Station Hill are distributed by Chicago-based Independent Publishers Group. Natus Books is dedicated to providing publication services to religious, political, community and cultural organizations.

About the Author

If fate—namely the failed Hungarian Revolution of 1956—had not intervened, Laszlo Z. Bito (1934-2021) would have become a fiction writer. However, because of his involvement as a local organizer, he was forced to flee Hungary and, upon his arrival in the United States—an immigrant without knowledge of English—choose a more practical career.

Bito graduated with a BA in chemistry and biology from Bard College and went on to earn a PhD in biophysics and cell biology from Columbia University. In 1965, he joined the Ophthalmology faculty of that university and worked in biomedical science. His research led to the development of the drug Xalatan, which for many years has been the gold standard in the treatment of glaucoma.

Bito retired from Columbia at the age of sixty-three to devote himself to writing. By the time of his death he had published more than twenty books in Hungarian; some were translated into German and several Eastern European languages. He produced, among other works, four books based on observations from his own experience, six biblical novels, and five anthologies of previously published essays and editorials. *The Gospel of Anonymous*, published in 2011, was his first, and until now only, novel published in English.